HOW TO MAKE
BEAUTIFUL
FOOD
IN A MOLD

HOW TO MAKE BEAUTIFUL FOOD IN A MOLD

by Ceil Dyer

David McKay Company, Inc.

NEW YORK

Library of Congress Cataloging in Publication Data

Dyer, Ceil.
How to make beautiful food in a mold.

Includes index.
1. Cookery (Molded dishes) I. Title.
TX740.D97 641.5'89 76-16208
ISBN 0-679-50607-1

Contents

Introduction

This book is the result of a long and continuing interest in an important, yet often neglected, method of cooking: preparing molded food. In this country, except for gelatin salads and desserts, molded foods are largely ignored. Over the years I have collected a wealth of recipes for molded dishes, the culinary creations of great chefs and fine cooks. Many of their recipes—and they are all given here—are, in fact, masterpieces (haute cuisine, no less). But don't let this deter your decision to prepare them. Each recipe has been simplified and modernized so that even the novice cook can make them successfully.

Despite the fact that all of these recipes are steamed, baked, chilled or frozen in a mold, the range and diversity of food is broad. There are elegant but hearty main course molds of meat, fish and poultry; mousses and festive molded salads; plus picture perfect vegetables that make even people who "hate" vegetables and salads ask for seconds. You'll find filling and nutritious rice molds, molded pasta dishes and the most beautiful way of presenting potatoes.

For desserts there are spectacular charlottes and superb but oh-so-easy steamed puddings; bombes and frozen mousses that will make your reputation as a dessert cook; and the most delightful and fanciful of molded cakes and cookies that are primer-book easy to make.

As mold cookery has its own vocabulary, though it's an easy one to learn, I have begun this book with a mini-dictionary of mold cookery terms. Even if you are an experienced and expert cook, you may find it a handy place to look up a few culinary techniques that apply specifically to this particular collection of recipes. I've tried to include everything anyone will need to know for unfailing success because mold cookery once mastered is, for so many reasons, a really great way to cook.

Molded dishes are problem solvers. With a few multipurpose molds in your kitchen plus the basic know-how you can transform inexpensive ingredients into expensive looking, rich-tasting dishes and present a tantalizing buffet supper even though food costs are spiraling and your budget is lagging woefully behind. You can put nourishing, appealing meals on the table even when you have very little time for preparation because you can cook ahead. Even those desolate-looking leftovers can be transformed into glorious mousses, delicate timbales, appetizing molded salads or a number of other satisfying molded dishes.

Molded dishes are, more often than not, quick and easy to prepare. There's no basting or turning, no repeated bending over a hot stove (as in broiling). Constant attention is not needed while the food cooks; there is no hot grease as in frying; and, unlike sautéing, there's very little stirring over heat.

What's more, though molded entrees look and taste as rich as sin, they are usually less fattening than fried or sautéed foods. Desserts, too, even when made with rich cream, nearly always contain fewer calories per portion than do pies or iced cakes.

The really big plus in this very versatile method of food preparation is that everything looks so tantalizing and tastes so very good.

If this book gives you a fresh approach to menu planning, if it expands your culinary horizons and makes your everyday cooking just a bit more adventurous, it will have accomplished its purpose. It will certainly please me, and I hope it will also please you. Cooking is such fun when it's easy. I think you'll find mold cookery just fits the bill—it's both easy and fun.

THE WORLD OF
MOLD COOKERY

Mold Glossary

Aspic

Originally, aspic referred only to a decorated dish coated with, or molded in, jelly. Today the word is used interchangeably for the prepared dish or jelly itself. Both aspic and jelly (*gelée* in French) are used to refer to the mixture in either the liquid or jellied state.

Broth, Bouillon, Stock

Most cookbooks use the words interchangeably, as a basic definition can apply to them all. They are the liquid obtained from simmering meats, poultry or fish with bones, vegetables, seasoning and water. This liquid, cooked down and strained, is the base used by gourmet cooks for sauces, soups and consommes. Clarified and sometimes fortified with commercial gelatin, it is used for aspic. A stock made with veal knuckle bones and beef or chicken bones will result in a firm jelly without additional gelatin. Canned broth, bouillon or stock plus unflavored gelatin can, of course, be substituted for the homemade, so all recipes in this book leave the choice to the cook.

Pâté

A mixture of meats and seasonings baked in a terrine (or loaf pan) that has been lined with thinly sliced pork fat or bacon.

Pâté en Croûte

Pâté mixture baked in crust in a pâté mold or loaf pan.

Mousse

In cooking, this term is used for a number of very different hot and cold dishes. There are savory mousses of fish, chicken or meat; and sweet mousses such as chocolate or fruit. There are frozen mousses made with a very rich custard base, and mousses made with ice cream embellished with liqueur, fruits or nuts. The only similarities which all mousses have in common are that they have a creamy smooth consistency and are made in molds.

Bombe Glacée

Originally a classic French bombe glacée was made in a spherical mold (hence the name) using two mousse mixtures of different flavors. In this country, bombes are usually prepared in decorative molds lined with ice cream, then filled with a rich mousse mixture or another flavor of ice cream.

Timbale

In French, the word *timbale* originally meant a sort of hot pie made in a high round mold and filled with forcemeats or various other kinds of meats. Then, to meet the needs of the ordinary home cook, timbale cases were made in fireproof porcelain in the shape and color of the real piecrust. In this country, timbales are usually a non-sweet custardlike mixture made in individual molds, turned out and served sans crust, but topped with some type of sauce. There are cheese timbales; ham, chicken or fish timbales; vegetable timbales, etc.

Timbales are as glamorous as soufflés and just as elegant and delicious. But unlike soufflés, they are not temperamental and are much less complicated to prepare.

Soufflés usually require a cream sauce base whereas timbales are most often made with eggs and cream or milk, and require no precooking. While timbales may seem the more delicate of the two, they decidedly are not; they are, in fact, much more hearty. Soufflés must be served as soon as they are baked; timbales, on the other hand, can be kept waiting in a warm oven for a considerable time. If necessary, they can even be steamed, kept at room temperature for several hours, then reheated without loss of texture.

Molds

They come in a variety of sizes and shapes. *Larousse Gastronomique (The French Dictionary of Food)* gives this definition: "a hollow receptacle made in different materials and different shapes used in cooking and confectionary." Some molds that can be used for recipes in this book are:

Charlotte mold

A straight-sided, deep mold used for Charlotte Russe. Can also be used for gelatin salads and desserts, mousses and frozen bombes.

Cylindrical mold

Tall, round nondecorative mold used for steamed breads and puddings.

Fish-shaped decorative mold

Especially for fish or seafood mousse—can also be used for gelatin salads or aspics.

Hinged decorative cake mold

Specialty molds of various designs geared to holiday motifs: bunnies, lambs, Santas, etc.

Kugelhupf mold

For classic fruit-filled yeast dough cake, but also for effective molded gelatin salads and desserts.

Madeleine mold

Shell-shaped, one- to three-inch molds grouped on a plaque, used for Madeleines—the rich little French cakes Proust made famous. Can also be used for preparing attractive gelatin shells for garnishing other dishes, as well as for making molded hard sauce as an elegant garnish with Christmas plum pudding.

Melon mold

Half-melon shaped mold for dessert mousses or bombes. Nice, too, for gelatin salads and desserts. Can be covered and used to prepare a very pretty steamed pudding.

Pâté mold

Hinged decorative mold, usually oblong or oval, especially designed for Pâté en Croûte.

Pudding mold

Decorative, fancy-shaped molds with lids for steamed puddings. Can also be used when preparing bombes, mousses, gelatin salads and desserts.

Ring mold

Versatile multiuse rings which come in various sizes and can be used for almost all molded dishes. Particularly effective when used for molds with accompanying sauces, which can be placed in the center of the ring.

Rosace mold

Multipurpose decorative round mold with a rose design on top, traditionally used for Rosace cake.

Savarin mold

Especially for Savarin cake. Named for Anthèlme Brillat-Savarin, a French politician, writer and gourmet, the Savarin

cake is a brioche baked in a ring mold and covered with fruit
and nuts. The ring mold is multipurpose and can be used for a
variety of baked or unbaked specialties.

Timbale cases

This term usually applies to nondecorative individual molds
that are custard cup size. Primarily used for cheese, vegetable
or chicken timbales, but may be used for individual portions of
salad or dessert.

Trois Frères mold

Multipurpose decorative mold named after three celebrated
Parisian cooks of the nineteenth century. Originally designed for
a special cake, it's swirled top is perfect for molded salads and
desserts, as well as bombes and frozen mousses.

Definition of Methods

Beating egg whites until stiff

Separate whites from yolks as soon as eggs are removed from refrigerator, since they separate more easily when they are cold. Let whites come to room temperature before beating. Use a wire whisk and a large deep bowl. The bowl should be neither aluminum, which will turn your whites an unpleasant gray, nor plastic, which often has a chemical that deters volume development. Be sure that both beater and bowl are completely free of grease, thoroughly clean and dry. Beat steadily, without stopping, until the whites hold firm peaks when the beater is lifted from the bowl. When this is achieved, the consistency will be what most cookbooks describe as "stiff, but not dry."

Folding beaten egg whites together with other ingredients

Purists will tell you that for best results you must fold the lighter ingredients—the egg whites—into the heavier ones—usually a sauce. However, this involves the added step of transferring the sauce from its saucepan to another bowl. I've found that the same good results can be achieved by stirring a small portion of the beaten whites into the sauce, then folding the thus lightened sauce into the egg whites.

Whipping cream

Thoroughly chill bowl, beater and cream by placing them in the freezer or freezer compartment of your refrigerator for about 15 minutes. This will reduce whipping time by about half. Use a large bowl and a wire whisk. Don't overbeat. The perfect state (for using in bombes, mousses, etc.) is reached when the cream will hold soft peaks and cling to the beater as it is lifted from the bowl. If the cream is too stiff and dry it will give the finished dish very dense texture.

To purée

To purée is to mash smooth as in mashed potatoes. You can purée foods through a food mill, through a fine sieve, in a mortar with a pestle or in an electric blender. With the blender method, you must be careful not to overblend and liquefy or to clog the blender with too dense a mixture. However, it is the easiest and quickest method and is used in this book. If your kitchen lacks this equipment, you can purée your ingredients by any of the above methods and obtain the same results.

To steam

Metal molds are used for steaming. These molds are called pudding molds and are available in various forms. But a coffee or lard can, a ring mold or any metal pan can be converted into such a mold. If the mold has no cover of its own, cover it with a layer of aluminum foil. The foil should overlap the top by one inch and be held tightly in place with a rubber band. No steam should be allowed to seep into the mold.

Technically, steaming means to cook over simmering water in a covered pot. The food is cooked by the resulting moist steam. Steamer pots are made especially for this purpose; however, puddings or other food cooked in a mold may be steamed successfully in any large heavy pot. Place the covered mold in the pot on a trivet or a crumpled round of foil, add sufficient hot water to cover bottom of pot, then cover the pot. The food will steam over the simmering water. This is the method used throughout the book because special steamer pots are not standard equipment in the average kitchen. More importantly, I have found the results the same as in classic steaming, and the procedure is easier and quicker.

Preparation of mold

The mold should be buttered and often sugared or floured according to recipe directions for mousses, timbales, steamed puddings, etc.

Grease generously with soft, spreadable butter, which is the only way to achieve a thick, even coating necessary for easy unmolding.

Place the mold in the refrigerator or freezer while preparing the recipe. The mold is chilled to firm the butter so that it will stay where it belongs, and the dish will turn out with ease—no ragged sides or top.

If the mold is to be sugared or floured, just before adding recipe mixture place a small amount of flour or sugar into the greased mold, cover and shake vigorously until all surfaces are lightly covered.

If the mold is to be steamed, it should not be filled more than two-thirds full. A mold of a larger capacity may be substituted for a smaller one. But remember never to fill a mold to the brim, or part of the ingredients will ooze out into the water.

To unmold and serve hot dishes (such as mousses, timbales, or ring molds)

Remove mold from the oven and let stand about 5 minutes. Run a knife around the inside edges of the mold and place a warm platter (or plate) upside down on top of it. Grasping platter and mold firmly together, invert them quickly. Rap the platter sharply on the work surface and the mousse (or whatever) should slide out easily. If desired, spoon sauce over surface and garnish platter appropriately for the dish.

To unmold frozen desserts

Remove mold from freezer and let stand at room temperature for about 5 minutes. Dip a small pointed knife in warm water and slide it around the rim to loosen the top edge. Then dip mold just to the rim in warm (not hot) water and hold it for about 10 seconds. Lift from water, place serving plate over mold and invert quickly. Carefully lift off the mold container. If dessert doesn't release easily, dip the mold in warm water a second time.

To unmold gelatin salads, mousses, entrees and desserts

Chill until firm and congealed—several hours or overnight.

Use a small pointed knife dipped in warm water to loosen top edge. Dip mold, just to the rim, in warm (not hot) water for about 10 seconds. Moisten the top of gelatin and a chilled serving plate with cold water. The moistened plate allows food to be moved on it after unmolding.

Place moistened plate over mold and invert. Carefully lift off mold container. If gel does not release easily, dip the mold in warm water once again.

Gelatin Terminology

Chill until slightly thickened

DEFINITION: Consistency of unbeaten egg whites.

USAGE: When folding a creamy mixture or ingredient such as cream cheese or whipped cream into gelatin.

Chill until thickened

DEFINITION: Spoon drawn through gelatin leaves a definite impression.

USAGE: When adding fruit, vegetables, or other solid ingredients to gelatin.

Set but not firm

DEFINITION: Gelatin sticks to finger when touched, and mounds or moves to side when tilted.

USAGE: When making fancy gelatin molds. This describes desired consistency of gelatin in mold when adding decorative food to form a design.

Firm

DEFINITION: Gelatin does not mound or move when mold is tilted and does not stick to finger.

USAGE: When gelatin is ready to be unmolded.

Equipment for Mold Cookery

Most kitchens have all of the "basics" for preparing molded foods, even the molds. Special ring molds, individual timbale molds and pudding molds with lids plus an assortment of decorative molds are nice to own—they make mold cookery more interesting and are popular for decorating kitchen walls.

However, you can prepare all sorts of molded dishes with the equipment you have on hand: a loaf pan is fine for patés—in fact, I prefer it to a classic hinged paté mold. With a loaf pan there's no danger of melted fat leaking to spoil my clean oven. Round-bottomed mixing bowls can be used for all sorts of jellied or frozen molded foods, as long as they can stand the extremes of temperature. Custard cups double as timbale molds and a one-pound coffee or shortening can serves successfully as a pudding mold and can be used for steamed breads and puddings.

Other necessary equipment?

If you own a saucepan and a double boiler, spoons for stirring, a chopping board and knife, you're on the way. Add to these a wire whisk for beating egg whites and heavy cream and an electric blender or a fine sieve to prepare puréed foods, and you are in business—or should I say pleasure—to make delectable molded appetizers, salads, hot and cold entrées, vegetables and desserts.

MEATS

PÂTÉS

Country Pâté

Hearty and versatile, this pâté can be served at luncheon, cocktail time or dinner. It keeps well—just wrap in foil, store in the refrigerator, and slice as needed.

For luncheon on the terrace: Serve slices of pâté, a good potato salad, sliced tomatoes and an inexpensive but hearty red wine. For cocktails: Slice pâté thinly, cut each slice in four and serve with cocktail rye rounds that have been spread lightly with Dijon mustard. For dinner: Serve as a first course with small sour pickles and watercress to garnish the plate.

2 pounds lean pork, coarsely chopped
1 pound veal, finely chopped
1½ pounds ground calves' liver
¼ pound fresh side pork or fat back, finely diced
3 eggs
4 cloves garlic, peeled and finely minced
¼ teaspoon freshly grated nutmeg
1 teaspoon mixed Italian herbs
1 tablespoon salt
1½ teaspoons freshly ground black pepper
½ cup whiskey or brandy
Salt pork or bacon slices to line the loaf pans

Line the bottoms of two 1-quart loaf pans with salt pork or bacon slices.

Preheat oven to 325°F.

Combine the meats, fat and eggs in a large bowl and knead together well with your hands. Add the seasonings and liquid, and blend well.

Add half of the meat mixture to each pan and smooth the surfaces. Top each with 2 slices of salt pork or bacon. Cover loosely with foil.

Bake in preheated oven for 1 hour. Remove foil and continue to bake another 1½ hours—a total of 2½ hours. (Note: The pâté will shrink from the sides when it is cooked.) Cool to room temperature.

Before refrigerating, cover tightly with foil or place in a plastic bag and fasten securely.

To serve, set pans in a shallow dish of very hot water for a moment to loosen and turn out onto a serving platter. Scrape off and discard surrounding fat. Using a sharp knife, cut the pâté into thin slices.

Serve with hot mustard and small sour pickles.

Makes 12 generous slices.

NOTE: Though a substantial quantity of fat is used, it ultimately becomes a thin coating on the pâté which is discarded before eating. The result is a lean, delicious, high protein appetizer or main course.

Curried Pâté

This is a very smooth textured pâté and a nice addition to a buffet menu. It looks very elegant on an oblong platter in a row of overlapping slices, the platter garnished with watercress and radish roses.

3 tablespoons butter	2–3 dashes hot pepper
1 tablespoon curry	sauce
powder	5 anchovy fillets, drained
3 tablespoons flour	and finely chopped
1½ cups chicken stock—	1 pound fresh calves'
either canned or	liver—or, as a sub-
homemade but free of	stitute, beef liver
all fat	¼ pound fresh pork fat
¼ cup cream	2 eggs, lightly beaten
¼ cup dry sherry	1 pound fresh pork fat—
1½ teaspoons salt	have your butcher cut
1 teaspoon pepper	it into long ⅛-inch-
½ teaspoon allspice	thick slices to line pans

Line a 1½- to 2-quart pâté pan or loaf pan with the sliced pork fat, reserving 2 slices for top of pâté. Place them crosswise and slightly overlapping to completely cover the bottom and sides of the pan. Set aside.

Preheat oven to 350°F.

In a saucepan melt the butter over low heat. Stir in the curry powder, then the flour. Slowly add ¾ cup of chicken stock, stirring as it is added. Stir in the cream and sherry. Continue to stir until the sauce is thick and smooth—6 to 7 minutes. Stir in salt, pepper, allspice, hot pepper sauce and chopped anchovies. Remove from heat. Cover sauce directly with plastic wrap and set aside at room temperature.

Dice the liver and pork fat into ½-inch pieces. Place in a skillet and cover with remaining stock. Simmer about 20 minutes. Drain. Place about ¼ of the meat mixture in the container of an electric blender. Add about ⅓ cup of the sauce and blend to a smooth purée. Transfer to a large mixing bowl. Repeat until all liver and pork have been puréed with sauce. Stir in any remaining sauce and beaten eggs. Spoon into fat-lined pâté or loaf pan, top with reserved pork fat slices. Cover pan with foil, sealing edges.

Place pan in a large baking dish and pour in sufficient hot water to come halfway up sides of the former .

Place on center rack of preheated oven and bake for 1½ hours. Remove from oven, remove foil and cool to room temperature. Again cover with foil and place a weight on top to press down the pâté—two or three magazines rolled and wrapped in foil will do nicely, as will an unopened can of coffee or any heavy can of food from your kitchen shelf.

Refrigerate the pâté for at least 6 hours or overnight.

Unmold onto serving plate. Slice and serve.

Serves 10 to 15 guests as a cocktail hors d'oeuvre or eight guests as a first course.

Grandmère's Jellied Liver Pâté

2½ pounds beef liver, sliced	2 teaspoons salt
½ pound pork liver, sliced	6 to 8 peppercorns
4 cups water	½ teaspoon sage
2 cloves garlic, peeled	¼ teaspoon thyme
1 small purple onion, peeled and quartered	½ teaspoon celery salt
1 or 2 leafy celery tops	⅛ teaspoon ground cloves
Sprig of parsley	⅛ teaspoon nutmeg
½ to ¾ cup fresh mushroom stems (Save the caps to stuff and serve as an elegant hors d'oeuvre.)	½ teaspoon seasoned salt
	2 envelopes unflavored gelatin
	½ cup Madeira

Chill a 1½- to 2-quart oblong mold or loaf pan.

Cover beef and pork livers with water in a large saucepan and bring to a boil. Skim surface until clear. Add garlic, onion, celery tops, parsley and mushroom stems. Season with salt and pepper. Reduce heat and simmer about 30 minutes until liver is tender.

Remove liver and chop coarsely. Strain stock and reserve 2½ cups.

Place liver and 1 cup of stock in container of electric blender and blend to a smooth purée. Transfer to a large mixing bowl. Add sage, thyme, celery salt, ground cloves, nutmeg and seasoned salt. Blend very thoroughly.

Sprinkle gelatin over Madeira and let stand several minutes to soften. Heat remaining 1½ cups of stock to boiling. Add softened gelatin and Madeira, and stir until dissolved. Add to liver mixture and again blend thoroughly. Cool to room temperature.

Rinse chilled mold with cold water. Transfer liver mixture to prepared mold. Chill until firm.

Unmold just before serving and garnish platter as desired. Serves 8 to 12.

Pâté Maison

Serve as an appetizer with drinks or as a first course for dinner. I nearly always take this pâté on a picnic, made in a two-cup round-bottomed bowl wrapped in foil and kept cold in an ice bucket. It's a successful addition to any alfresco menu.

1 pound best quality liverwurst at room temperature
¼ pound butter at room temperature
2 tablespoons Sauce Diable or Sauce Robert or the mixture of 1 teaspoon prepared mustard, 1 teaspoon Worcestershire sauce and 1 tablespoon heavy cream

¼ cup cognac or good, dry brandy

Lightly grease six ½-cup individual decorative molds or small timbale molds.

Combine first four ingredients and mix together until smooth and thoroughly blended.

Pack molds firmly with pâté mixture and chill several hours.

Unmold and serve with small sour pickles and unsalted crackers. If refrigerated, mold will keep five to six days.

Serves 6 as a first course; 8 to 10 as a cocktail hors d'oeuvre.

ASPICS

Cold Braised Beef in Wine Aspic

Except for the additional gelatin that is used to insure a firm jelly, this is a classic French recipe. Though there are several steps involved in its preparation, it's very easy to make. As it tastes so superb, I think you will find it well worth the time involved. It makes a perfect dish for a buffet supper party.

1 beef rump or top
round of beef, 4½ to
5 pounds
2 teaspoons salt mixed
with 1 teaspoon freshly
ground black pepper
1 large purple onion,
peeled and sliced
2 cloves garlic, peeled
and chopped
2 bay leaves, crumbled
2 cups dry red wine

¼ cup corn or safflower
oil
2 tablespoons apple
cider vinegar
¼ pound salt pork
¼ cup brandy
1 pig's foot, cut up
1 cup beef stock or
broth
¼ cup Madeira
3 envelopes unflavored
gelatin
½ cup cold water

Rub the meat with the salt and pepper mixture. Place it in a large glass or earthenware bowl. Sprinkle over it the onion, garlic and bay leaves.

Mix together the wine, oil and vinegar. Pour over meat and vegetables.

Cover bowl and refrigerate for 12 to 24 hours, turning meat occasionally.

Remove bowl from refrigerator and let stand in marinade at

room temperature for an additional 2 to 4 hours. Meat should be at room temperature before cooking process begins.

Dice salt pork, place in a small pan and cover with water. Bring water to boil, then lower heat and simmer for about 5 minutes. Drain and pat thoroughly dry with paper toweling.

Fry the blanched, diced pork in a large heavy Dutch oven or enameled cast-iron skillet over moderate heat until pork is brown and crisp. Remove from the melted fat with a slotted spoon and discard.

Remove the room temperature meat from the marinade and pat it thoroughly dry with paper toweling. Strain and reserve the marinade. Reheat the rendered pork fat to almost the smoking point and add the meat. Now reduce the heat so that the meat browns evenly without burning. Turn it often so that all sides brown gradually rather than each side browning completely before being turned.

When the beef is a deep mahogany brown all over, turn off the heat. Remove meat, pour off all but about 1 tablespoon of fat, then return meat to pot.

In a small skillet heat the brandy until warm. Reheat the meat until the fat begins to sizzle. Pour in the brandy and set it alight. Shake the pot gently until the flame dies out.

Now add the pig's foot and pour in the beef stock or broth and strained marinade.

Bring liquid to a full boil, then lower heat and loosely cover pot. Simmer over low heat on top of the stove for 3½ to 4 hours, or until meat is very tender. Turn the meat several times as it cooks.

Remove meat from liquid and let cool slightly, then wrap in plastic wrap and refrigerate. Strain liquid into a bowl and refrigerate until fat congeals—several hours or overnight.

Cut the chilled meat into thin slices with a sharp knife and arrange in a 2½- to 3-quart mold.

Remove and discard fat from surface of stock. Reheat stock and add Madeira.

Sprinkle gelatin over cold water to soften. Then stir softened gelatin into simmering stock and stir until dissolved. Pour over meat slices.

Cover and refrigerate until stock has jellied and is thoroughly chilled.

Unmold onto serving platter. This can be done 1 to 2 hours before serving, but keep refrigerated until serving time.

Serves 10 to 12.

Deviled Beef in Aspic

An excellent way to use leftover roast beef or pot roast. If you do not have sufficient meat on hand, you can "add to" with delicatessen roast beef; or, if it's less expensive (and it often is), use boiled tongue.

2 envelopes unflavored gelatin

1½ cups beef stock or broth

½ cup port wine

1 tablespoon prepared mustard

1 teaspoon Worcestershire sauce

3 or 4 dashes Tabasco sauce

½ cup chopped mixed pickles

½ cup finely chopped celery

¼ cup finely chopped radishes

¼ cup finely chopped green pepper

2 cups cooked roast beef, finely diced

MAYONNAISE COLÉE (optional)—see Sauces and Accompaniments

Chill a 2-quart mold or loaf pan.

Sprinkle gelatin over ½ cup of the beef stock or broth to soften.

Heat remaining beef stock and port wine just to boiling point. Stir in softened gelatin and liquid. Remove from heat and stir until gelatin has dissolved. Stir in mustard, Worcestershire sauce and Tabasco sauce. Cool at room temperature, then refrigerate until mixture begins to thicken—about 15 minutes. Fold in remaining ingredients.

Rinse chilled mold with cold water. Pour in beef mixture and refrigerate for several hours until firm.

Unmold onto lettuce-lined serving platter and garnish with tomato wedges and sliced cucumber. Or unmold and "ice" with MAYONNAISE COLÉE. Decorate with pimento strips and slivers of black olives.

Makes 6 to 8 buffet servings.

LOAVES

Ham Loaf

You can make this a very elegant buffet dish if you "ice" the loaf completely with MAYONNAISE COLÉE. Serve on a bed of watercress. Garnish the platter with tomato wedges, radish roses, pickle fans and small pickled beets.

¾ pound sliced smoked ham	2 tablespoons horseradish
1 medium sized cold boiled potato	3 egg whites
¾ cup milk (more if needed)	HORSERADISH SAUCE, MUSTARD SAUCE or MAYONNAISE COLÉE— see Sauces and Accompaniments
3 egg yolks	
½ pint heavy cream	
2 tablespoons catsup	

Grease a 1½-quart oblong mold or loaf pan with oil. Invert on paper toweling to remove excess oil. Line the bottom and ends of mold with aluminum foil, letting the foil extend over both ends by about ½ inch, and grease foil lightly with oil.

Preheat oven to 350°F.

Chop the ham into 1-inch pieces, discarding bones and fat. Peel and chop the potato.

In container of electric blender place milk and egg yolks. Blend at low speed for just 1 second. Add ham, potatoes, heavy cream, catsup and horseradish. Blend at high speed until mixture is a smooth, thick purée. If blender clogs, add a little additional milk. (Turn off motor and stir milk into other ingredients, then continue blending.) Transfer purée to a mixing bowl.

In a separate bowl beat egg whites until stiff. Beat in a little of the ham mixture, then fold into ham mixture until there are no remaining streaks of white.

Spoon into prepared mold. Place in a baking pan and pour in sufficient hot water to come about halfway up sides of mold.

Bake on middle rack of preheated oven for about 1 hour, or until firm.

Loosen sides of loaf from mold with a knife; then, with the help of the foil at the ends of mold, gently lift loaf out and invert onto serving platter. Remove foil.

Serve with HORSERADISH or MUSTARD SAUCE or MAYONNAISE COLÉE.

Serves 4.

Spiced Cider Ham Loaf

1 cup seedless raisins	¼ cup light brown sugar
3½ cups unsweetened apple juice	3 whole cloves
3 envelopes unflavored gelatin	2 cups lean baked or boiled ham, finely minced
¼ cup Calvados or apple cider	

Rinse a 2-quart loaf pan and place in refrigerator to chill. Soak raisins in the apple juice until plump—about ½ hour. Sprinkle gelatin over Calvados or apple cider to soften. Drain raisins, reserving apple juice in a saucepan. Add brown sugar and cloves to apple juice and heat to boiling. Remove from heat, add softened gelatin and stir until dissolved. Remove and discard cloves. Pour into a mixing bowl. Cool, then refrigerate until mixture begins to thicken. Fold ham and raisins into thickened gelatin.

Rinse chilled mold with cold water. Pour in ham mixture and refrigerate for several hours until firm.

Unmold onto chilled platter.

Serves 6 to 8.

Curried Lamb Loaf

3 tablespoons butter
1 medium mild purple
　onion, peeled and
　minced
1 stalk celery, minced
1 tablespoon curry
　powder
½ cup chicken stock or
　broth

1½ pounds ground lean
　lamb, shoulder or
　shank
¼ pound ground pork
　sausage meat
1 cup soft bread crumbs
2 eggs, lightly beaten

Generously grease a pâté pan or a loaf pan. Line bottom and ends of loaf pan with aluminum foil, letting foil extend over ends by about ½ inch. Grease foil.

Preheat oven to 375°F.

Melt the butter in a small saucepan. Stir in the onion and celery. Sauté until limp. Add curry powder and stir for a few seconds. Remove from heat and stir in stock or broth.

In a large bowl mix together the ground lamb, ground sausage and bread crumbs. Add the beaten eggs and the curried stock mixture. Blend thoroughly.

Pack the mixture into the prepared pan.

Place on middle rack of preheated oven and bake for about 1 hour and 15 minutes, or until surface is well browned and the loaf shrinks from the sides of the pan.

Unmold onto serving platter.

Serves 6 to 8.

Classic Jellied Veal Loaf

2 *pounds meaty shank of veal*	1 *carrot, scraped and quartered*
2 *pounds veal shoulder*	¼ *to* ½ *cup mushroom stems (optional)*
1 *pound lean pork*	2 *cloves garlic, peeled*
2 *quarts water*	2 *teaspoons salt*
1 *large onion, peeled and quartered*	2 *bay leaves*
	1 *cup dry white wine*

Place veal shank and shoulder in a large, deep, heavy pot (enameled cast-iron is best). Add water and bring to a boil. Skim surface to remove brown foam. Add all remaining ingredients except wine. Bring to a full boil, then lower heat and simmer for about 2 hours. Add wine and continue to cook over low heat for about ½ hour, or until meat is very tender.

Remove bones from meat and reserve. Place in a large bowl and cool to room temperature. Add about 1 cup of the cooking liquid. Cover and refrigerate until ready to use.

Strain remaining cooking stock, add reserved bones, and simmer until reduced to about 7 cups liquid. Remove and discard bones. Pour stock into a large bowl. Cool slightly, then refrigerate 6 to 8 hours, or until fat has risen to the surface and stock has congealed.

Remove and discard fat from surface of stock and transfer congealed stock to a large pot. Also add stock drained from meat.

Remove any fat from meat, chop meat finely and add to stock. Bring meat and stock to a boil over medium heat. Reduce heat and simmer for about 5 minutes.

Pour meat and stock into two 1½-quart molds or loaf pans. Cover and refrigerate 6 to 8 hours, or overnight.

Unmold onto chilled serving platter.

Serves 8 to 10.

Pain de Veau en Couronne Managrère
(Home-Style Veal Loaf)

1 pound lean shoulder of veal—have your butcher grind meat twice

1 pound country-style spicy sausage meat— have your butcher grind meat twice

2 tablespoons butter

1 small white onion, peeled and chopped

2 cloves garlic, peeled

2 or 3 sprigs parsley, chopped

3 eggs

¼ cup Madeira or dry sherry

1½ to 1¾ cups soft bread crumbs

Salt

Pepper

¼ teaspoon allspice

Salt pork or bacon slices to line mold

GLAZED CARROTS AND ONIONS —see Sauces and Accompaniments

Line a 2-quart ring mold or loaf pan with salt pork or bacon slices.

Preheat oven to 350°F.

Combine meats in a large mixing bowl.

Melt butter, but do not allow to brown.

Place melted butter, onion, garlic, parsley, eggs and Madeira or sherry in container of electric blender. Blend at high speed until smooth. Pour over meats and blend well. Add sufficient bread crumbs to make a soft, moist mixture that will just hold together. Salt and pepper to taste.

Spoon into prepared mold. Place mold in a baking pan and pour in sufficient hot water to come ¾ up sides of mold.

Place in preheated oven and bake for 1 hour, until firm.

Remove the mold from the oven and let stand 2 to 3 minutes. Loosen edges with a spatula and turn out onto a heated serving platter. Remove and discard salt pork or bacon slices. Fill center of mold with GLAZED CARROTS AND ONIONS. Serve with currant jelly.

Serves 6 to 8.

RING MOLDS

Tamale Hamburger Ring Mold

If you like Mexican food, you'll like this dish. It's great for an "easy-to-bring-to-the-table" Saturday night supper party. Just add a big green salad and buttered hot tortillas (frozen ones are absolutely great). Provide cold, cold beer or cola drinks. For dessert, serve the traditional Mexican cream cheese in guava shells.

1½ pounds hamburger—
    have your butcher
    grind meat twice
½ cup butter
1 tablespoon grated
    onion
1½ cups soft bread crumbs
2 tablespoons chili
    powder (less or more
    as desired)
1½ teaspoons salt

½ cup tomato juice
1 1-pound can tamales
1 1-pound can red
    kidney beans
1 1-pound can chili
    without beans
1 cup grated Monterey
    Jack or American brick
    cheese
½ cup minced parsley

Generously grease a 2-quart ring mold with a mixture of mild oil and butter. Set aside.

Preheat oven to 375°F.

In a large bowl mix together the meat, butter, onion, bread crumbs, chili powder, salt and tomato juice. Blend thoroughly; you can do this best with your hands.

Press about two-thirds of mixture into bottom and sides of mold.

Remove husks from tamales and cut each into thick (about 1½-inch) slices. Place slices upright, about 1 inch apart, over meat mixture. Pack meat mixture between tamale slices, then cover completely with remaining meat mixture.

Place mold on middle rack of preheated oven and bake for 45 to 50 minutes, or until the top is lightly browned and the meat shrinks from the sides of the mold.

While mold bakes, drain beans, combine with chili and heat thoroughly.

Unmold meat ring onto a serving platter. Fill center with chili and beans. Sprinkle with cheese and parsley, and serve at once.

Serves 6 to 8.

Italian Lamb and Eggplant Mold

The Italian seasoning in this originally Greek recipe gives it just the extra flavor needed. It's a beautiful dish and though it sounds difficult to make, it is actually very easy.

3 medium-sized eggplants	*1 cup Italian tomato sauce*
4 tablespoons butter	*1 teaspoon tomato paste*
2 onions, peeled and minced	*1 teaspoon mixed Italian herbs*
1 clove garlic, peeled and minced	*2 eggs, well beaten*
1½ pounds lean ground lamb (Note: Finely minced leftover cooked lamb may be substituted, if desired.)	

Grease a 1½-quart ring mold with oil. Invert onto paper toweling to drain. Set aside.

Preheat oven to 400°F.

With a small, sharp knife make several gashes about ½-inch deep and 1-inch long in each eggplant. Place them on middle rack of preheated oven and bake for about 1 hour, or until very soft.

While still warm cut each eggplant lengthwise into quarters and, using a spoon, scrape the pulp into a mixing bowl. Set aside. Reserve skins.

Reduce oven heat to 375°F.

Melt the butter in a large skillet. Add the onion and garlic and sauté until limp. Stir in the lamb and cook, stirring, until no longer pink. Blend in tomato sauce, tomato paste, herbs and eggplant pulp. Cook, stirring, until mixture is blended and thick but not dry. Remove from heat, cool slightly, then stir in beaten eggs.

Line the greased mold with the eggplant skins, purple side down. They should overlap the rim edges so that they may be folded over the filling.

Fill lined mold with the meat mixture and fold the skins over so they meet in the center and over the top. Place the mold in a shallow baking pan and add sufficient hot water to come halfway up sides of mold.

Place in preheated oven and bake for 45 to 50 minutes, or until firm.

Remove from oven and allow to stand at room temperature for about 5 minutes.

Unmold onto heated platter and serve with a tasty tomato sauce.

Serves 6 to 8.

MOUSSES

Corned Beef Mousse with Mustard Sauce

I like to serve this cold mousse with old-fashioned baked beans hot from the oven. It makes a hearty and filling buffet supper. Both the mousse and the beans are made one day ahead. I add a green salad and serve crusty French bread. The beverage is ice cold beer.

2 envelopes unflavored gelatin
1⅓ cups beef or chicken stock
1 1-pound can corned beef at room temperature
½ cup well-drained, mixed sweet pickles, finely minced

1 tablespoon prepared mustard
2 tablespoons strained lemon juice
½ cup sour cream
MUSTARD SAUCE—see Sauces and Accompaniments

Chill a 1½-quart ring mold or a loaf pan.

Sprinkle gelatin over ⅓ cup of stock to soften.

Heat remaining stock to boiling and stir in the softened gelatin. Chill until slightly thickened.

Place corned beef in a large bowl, mash and flake as finely as possible. Blend in pickles, mustard, lemon juice, thickened gelatin and sour cream.

Rinse chilled mold with cold water. Pour mixture into mold. Chill until firm—2 to 3 hours.

Unmold, garnish platter and serve with MUSTARD SAUCE.

Makes 4 to 6 servings.

Cold Ham Mousse with Mustard Mayonnaise

1 envelope unflavored gelatin	2 tablespoons chili sauce
⅓ cup cold water	1 tablespoon mustard
1 cup chicken stock or broth	2 tablespoons Madeira or dry sherry
2 cups lean baked or boiled ham, finely minced	½ cup heavy cream
	MUSTARD SAUCE—see Sauces and Accompaniments

Grease a 1-quart ring mold with mild oil, then invert on paper toweling to drain.

Sprinkle gelatin over cold water to soften.

Heat stock or broth to boiling and stir in softened gelatin. Stir over low heat until gelatin has dissolved. Pour into a large mixing bowl and refrigerate until chilled and just beginning to thicken. Stir frequently to insure even consistency. When ready to use, it should be quite thick, but still liquid.

Add minced ham, chili sauce, mustard and wine.

Stir to blend.

In a separate bowl, beat the cream until thick enough to cling lightly to the beater when it is lifted out of the bowl. Fold into ham mixture.

Pour mixture into prepared mold and refrigerate until firm— at least 4 hours.

Unmold onto a chilled platter.

Fill center of ring with MUSTARD SAUCE. Garnish as desired with gherkins, tomato wedges and cucumber slices.

Serves 4 to 6.

Hawaiian Ham and Pork Mousse with Pineapple

1½ pounds lean ground
    pork—have your
    butcher put pork
    through meat grinder
    twice
  1 cup (firmly packed)
    very finely minced,
    lean, leftover baked
    ham or ½ pound
    ground lean smoked
    ham
  ¼ cup very finely minced
    ham fat from leftover
    baked ham or from
    any smoked ham
  1 cup soft bread crumbs
  ½ cup milk

  ¼ cup canned, un-
    sweetened pineapple
    juice
  2 tablespoons catsup
  1 tablespoon horse-
    radish
  1 tablespoon prepared
    mustard
  2 tablespoons light
    brown sugar
Thin slices of ham fat from
    baked ham, thin slices
    of salt pork, or sliced
    bacon fat
Canned unsweetened pine-
    apple chunks or fresh
    pineapple chunks

Line the bottom and sides of a 2-quart ring mold with slices of ham fat, salt pork or bacon fat, pressing them down and together to form a complete lining.

Preheat oven to 350°F.

Combine first ten ingredients in a large mixing bowl and using a heavy wooden spoon, blend together thoroughly.

Spoon pork and ham mixture into mold and press it down evenly. Place a few slices of ham fat, salt pork or bacon fat over surface of pork mixture.

Place mold on middle rack of preheated oven and bake for 1½ hours.

Unmold and remove fat slices. Fill center of ring with pineapple and serve hot or at room temperature.

Serves 8 to 10.

Mousse de Veau
(Classic French-Style Veal Mousse)

2 *pounds lean ground*	1 *teaspoon salt*
veal—have your	½ *teaspoon white pepper*
butcher grind the meat	3 *egg whites*
twice	½ *pint heavy cream*
1 *small white onion*	2 *tablespoons Madeira*

Grease a 1½-quart oblong mold or loaf pan with oil. Invert onto paper toweling to drain excess oil. Line the bottom and ends of the mold or pan with aluminum foil letting the foil extend over both ends by about ½ inch. Lightly grease foil.

Preheat oven to 350°F.

Place the meat in a large mixing bowl and set bowl in a larger container of ice cubes. Using a hand grater, grate the onion over it. Add salt and pepper. Blend lightly, then add the unbeaten egg whites using an electric mixer or a large, heavy wooden spoon. Beat the mixture until well blended. Gradually add the cream, about 2 tablespoons at a time, beating well after each addition. When all cream is added, mixture should be light and very smooth. Stir in Madeira.

Spoon into prepared mold. Place in a baking pan and pour sufficient hot water around mold to come halfway up sides.

Bake on middle rack of preheated oven for about 50 minutes, or until firm.

Remove from oven and let stand at room temperature about 5 minutes before unmolding. Run a knife along both sides of mold. Gently lift ends of foil to loosen bottom of mousse, then turn out onto serving platter. Remove foil.

Serve with a good, rich tomato sauce, hollandaise sauce, cream sauce or creamed vegetables.

Serves 6 to 8.

TIMBALES

Ham Timbales with Mushroom Sauce

3 tablespoons butter
1 tablespoon minced onion
½ cup soft bread crumbs
1 cup lean baked or boiled ham, finely diced
1 cup cooked green peas

4 eggs
1 tablespoon tomato paste or catsup
1½ cups milk
MUSHROOM SAUCE—see Sauces and Accompaniments

Generously butter 6 individual timbale molds or custard cups. Preheat oven to 350°F.

Melt butter in a large skillet. Add onion and sauté until limp. Remove from heat and stir in bread crumbs, ham and peas.

In a mixing bowl beat eggs with tomato paste and milk until blended. Add ham mixture to egg mixture. Blend and pour into prepared molds.

Place molds in a baking pan and pour in sufficient water to come halfway up sides of mold.

Bake on middle rack of preheated oven for 25 to 30 minutes, or until firm.

Unmold and serve with MUSHROOM SAUCE.

Serves 6.

Ham and Vegetable Timbales

4 eggs

1½ cups milk or part milk, part fat-free chicken stock, canned or homemade

½ to ¾ cup lean baked or boiled ham, minced

½ to ¾ cup finely chopped, drained and blotted dry cooked carrots or cooked tiny green peas; or a combination of both vegetables

½ teaspoon grated onion

Salt, if needed (The ham may be sufficiently salty to season the mixture.)

Generously grease six ¾- to 1-cup timbale molds with soft butter. Chill.

Preheat oven to 350° F.

In a mixing bowl beat eggs with a wire whisk until frothy. Add milk or milk mixture and beat until blended. Add remaining ingredients and pour into prepared molds.

Place filled molds in a baking dish and pour sufficient hot water into dish to come halfway up sides of molds.

Bake in preheated oven until firm—about 25 minutes.

Unmold and serve with cheese sauce, tomato sauce, or with creamed mushrooms.

Serves 6.

VARIATIONS: For VEGETABLE TIMBALES omit ham. Use instead 1 to 1½ cups any chopped cooked vegetables on hand, such as mushrooms, green beans, cauliflower, etc. Use 1 tablespoon grated Parmesan cheese instead of the grated onion, if desired. Especially good served with crisp bacon or little link sausages.

POULTRY

PÂTÉS

Chicken Liver Pâté
Strasbourg Style

Not quite as rich and velvety smooth as a genuine Strasbourg pâté de foie gras, but a pâté with superb flavor and sufficiently elegant to present to your most distinguished guests.

1 pound chicken livers
1 thick slice purple
onion, peeled
1 small tart apple, peeled
and cored
4 tablespoons butter
¼ cup Madeira or
brandy

2 tablespoons Escoffier
Sauce Diable and 2
tablespoons heavy
cream, or 3½ table-
spoons heavy cream
and 1 teaspoon steak
sauce
½ pound very soft but
not melted butter

Cut away all gristle and any green or brown spots from the chicken livers. Place them in a colander and rinse under cold water. Turn out onto paper towels and blot thoroughly dry.

Mince the onion and apple, or grate on the coarse side of a hand grater.

Melt 2 tablespoons of butter in a skillet, add onion and apple, and sauté over low heat until apple is soft enough to mash with a wooden spoon. Scrape entire contents of skillet into container of electric blender.

Wipe skillet clean with paper toweling. Add remaining 2 table-spoons of butter and melt over low heat. Add chicken livers and cook, stirring often, until lightly browned through center. (To test cut one in half.)

Add chicken livers and cooking butter to onion-apple mixture in blender. Add Madeira or brandy. Then add cream and Sauce

Diable, or cream and steak sauce. Blend at high speed until as smooth as thick cream. Add a little additional cream if mixture is too thick. Turn out into a mixing bowl. Add butter a little at a time, blending well after each addition.

When all butter has been added and mixture is smooth, pack into a 1- to 2-cup earthenware mold. Smooth surface of pâté and cover directly with plastic wrap. Refrigerate 6 to 8 hours.

Unmold and serve with thinly sliced French bread, homemade melba toast or unsalted crackers.

Serves 8 to 10 as a cocktail hors d'oeuvre, 6 to 8 as a first course.

ASPICS

Chicken Liver Pâté in Aspic

If you want to serve something elegant but inexpensive and easy to make at your next cocktail party, you might consider this favorite pâté.

PÂTÉ

½ pound butter
1 small onion, peeled and chopped
½ small clove garlic, peeled and minced
1 pound chicken livers
¼ cup Madeira or good, dry brandy

½ teaspoon dry mustard
¼ teaspoon salt
1 tablespoon Escoffier Sauce Diable, or substitute 1 teaspoon Worcestershire sauce

ASPIC

1 envelope unflavored gelatin
¼ cup cold water

1 cup clear chicken stock or broth, free of all fat

GARNISH

Thin strips of well-drained pimento

Black olive slivers

Lightly grease a 1-quart decorative mold with corn oil; invert on paper toweling to drain off excess oil. Refrigerate until ready to use.

Place ¼ cup (½ stick) butter in a saucepan over medium heat. When melted add the onion and garlic, and sauté until limp.

Add chicken livers and another ¼ cup of butter. Stir and cook over low heat until livers are firm and no longer pink in center. (Test by cutting one in half.)

Remove from heat and add the Madeira or brandy. Stir in the mustard, salt and Sauce Diable or Worcestershire sauce. Cut remaining butter into small pieces and add to mixture. Place about ⅓ of mixture at a time in container of electric blender and blend at high speed to a very smooth purée, but do not overblend. Scrape into a mixing bowl and place in refrigerator while preparing aspic. Mixture should be cold before using.

To prepare aspic:

Sprinkle gelatin over cold water in a small bowl to soften.

Heat chicken stock to boiling, and add softened gelatin. Stir over low heat until gelatin is completely dissolved.

Remove from heat and pour into a well-chilled, small metal bowl. Refrigerate until chilled and thickened.

To prepare pâté in aspic:

Place chilled mold in a bowl of ice cubes and spoon some of the chilled, thickened-but-still-liquid aspic into it, then turn the mold so that the jelly runs around the sides and covers the bottom. Push the mold down into the bowl of ice so that it is surrounded by ice cubes. When the aspic is almost firm, repeat two or three times until the mold is completely lined with a "shell" of the aspic. Refrigerate until aspic is almost set and feels "sticky" to the touch.

Dip strips of pimento and olive slivers in remaining thick, chilled-but-still-liquid aspic, and arrange in aspic-lined mold. Again refrigerate mold until aspic is set but still feels slightly "sticky."

Fill with chilled chicken liver pâté. Pour any remaining liquid aspic over surface. Cover and refrigerate several hours before unmolding.

Unmold onto a chilled platter.

Serves 10 to 12 as cocktail hors d'oeuvre, 6 to 8 as a first course.

NOTE: If the aspic becomes too stiff to handle at any point, reheat briefly, then chill to correct consistency before proceeding.

Turkey and Smithfield Ham in Aspic

2 cups fat-free chicken
  stock, canned or
  homemade
1 cup dry white wine
1 medium onion, peeled
  and quartered
2 cloves garlic, peeled
  and split in half
  lengthwise
1 stalk celery with leaves
2 or 3 parsley sprigs

1 2-inch strip lemon
  peel
12 black peppercorns
2 envelopes unflavored
  gelatin
⅓ cup cold water
2 cups boned, skinned,
  coarsely chopped left-
  over roast turkey
1 4-ounce jar Smithfield
  ham spread

Chill a 1-quart mold or loaf pan.

Combine first eight ingredients in a saucepan and bring to a boil. Lower heat and simmer very gently for about 30 minutes.

Strain through a fine sieve, compressing vegetables with the back of a wooden spoon to extract all liquid.

Measure the strained stock. There should be about 2 cups. If less, add additional stock; if more, boil down to desired quantity.

Soften the gelatin in ⅓ cup water.

Reheat strained stock. Add softened gelatin to hot stock and stir over low heat until dissolved. Refrigerate until thoroughly chilled and thickened but still liquid.

In a mixing bowl combine chopped turkey and Smithfield ham and mix together gently but thoroughly.

Rinse chilled mold with cold water. Pack the mixture, not too firmly, into the prepared mold. Slowly pour the stock over it and shake the mold gently to distribute the stock evenly throughout. Pour in just enough to cover the turkey mixture. Pour any remaining stock into a shallow pan to be chilled until firm. Then chop and use as garnish. Chill mold for several hours until firm.

Unmold onto a chilled plate and garnish with sliced pimento-stuffed olives, sprigs of watercress and chopped jellied aspic.

Serves 6.

VARIATION: Freshly boiled chicken can be substituted for the turkey. You can also eliminate the ham spread and use instead 1 cup leftover freshly cooked chicken or turkey and 1 cup chopped lean boiled or baked ham.

LOAVES

Chicken Loaf

This dish is perfect for a buffet supper.

3 envelopes unflavored gelatin	½ cup cold water
½ cup dry white wine	¾ cup mayonnaise
1 cup chicken broth or stock	1 to 1½ cups diced cooked chicken or turkey
1 hard-cooked egg, thinly sliced	1 cup finely diced celery
6 to 8 pimento-stuffed olives, thinly sliced	½ cup chopped pimento-stuffed olives
	½ cup chopped walnuts

Chill a 1½-quart loaf pan.

Sprinkle 1 envelope of gelatin over the wine in a small bowl. Let stand several minutes to soften. Heat chicken stock to boiling, pour over softened gelatin and stir until dissolved. Chill until the mixture thickens.

Rinse chilled mold with cold water. Pour in a thin layer of the thickened gelatin. Arrange sliced hard-cooked egg and sliced pimento-stuffed olives in a decorative pattern over surface. Chill until firm.

Return remaining gelatin and wine mixture to refrigerator and chill until firm.

Sprinkle remaining 2 envelopes of gelatin over cold water in top of double boiler. Stir over low heat until dissolved. Stir into mayonnaise in a medium sized bowl. Add remaining ingredients and blend well. Spoon into aspic-lined mold. Chill until firm.

Unmold onto chilled platter.

Dice remaining chilled aspic and use to garnish chicken loaf platter.

Serves 6.

Jellied Turkey Loaf with Cranberry Topping

TURKEY LOAF

2 envelopes unflavored
gelatin
2 chicken bouillon cubes
1 small white onion,
peeled and quartered
1 small clove garlic,
peeled
¾ cup boiling water

1 cup diced cooked
turkey
½ teaspoon salt
¼ teaspoon pepper
¼ teaspoon dried
tarragon
2 tablespoons dry sherry
1 cup heavy cream

Chill a 2-quart loaf pan.

Place gelatin, bouillon cubes, onion and garlic in container of electric blender. Add boiling water, cover and blend at high speed for 40 seconds.

Add remaining ingredients. Cover and blend at same speed for 10 seconds.

Rinse chilled mold with cold water. Pour in turkey mixture. Chill until firm.

CRANBERRY TOPPING

¼ cup cold water
1 envelope unflavored
gelatin
1 3-ounce package cherry
gelatin
1 cup boiling water

1 chopped orange,
peeled and seeded
with all white removed
Rind of 1 orange
1 1-pound can whole
cranberry sauce

Put cold water in container of electric blender, add gelatins and boiling water. Cover and blend at high speed for 40 seconds. Add orange and rind. Blend until rind is finely chopped. Add cranberry sauce. Cover and blend at same speed for 10 seconds.

Pour into loaf pan over jellied turkey and chill until set.

Unmold onto a lettuce lined platter. Serve with mayonnaise. Serves 4 to 6.

Steamed Turkey Loaf

This is a good and easy way to use up the bits and pieces of leftover roast turkey that are too small to use for any other purpose, as well as the leftover dressing and turkey gravy.

2 cups (leftover) crumbled turkey stuffing or sufficient leftover turkey stuffing and Pepperidge Farm turkey stuffing mix to total 2 cups

1 to 1½ cups finely diced turkey meat

½ cup chopped walnuts (optional)

1 to 2 tablespoons cranberry sauce

3 eggs, lightly beaten

Chicken stock or thin turkey gravy (If the gravy is "no longer," use canned gravy spiked with Madeira or sherry.)

Salt, if needed

Generously grease a 1½-quart cylindrical pudding mold and inside of lid with soft butter. Chill.

Combine turkey stuffing (or turkey stuffing and stuffing mix) with turkey meat and walnuts. Add cranberry sauce and eggs. Mix, then add sufficient stock or gravy to make a stiff but quite moist mixture. Taste and add salt, if needed.

Spoon into pudding mold. Cover mold and place on a rack in a large pot. Pour in sufficient hot water to cover the bottom of the pot by about 2 inches. Cover pot and steam loaf over medium heat until firm—about 1 hour.

Unmold and slice. Serve with leftover turkey gravy and slices of jellied cranberry sauce.

Serves 4 to 6.

MOLDS

Chicken or Turkey Ring Mold

3 tablespoons butter	½ teaspoon salt
2 tablespoons finely minced scallions or mild white onion	¼ teaspoon cayenne
	½ teaspoon paprika
	1 tablespoon lemon juice
1 pound fresh mushrooms, finely chopped (about 1 cup)	1½ cups finely chopped cooked turkey or chicken meat
2 tablespoons Madeira	¼ cup fine dry bread crumbs
3 tablespoons flour	
1 cup chicken or turkey stock, homemade or canned	2 egg whites
	CUMBERLAND SAUCE—see Sauces and Accompaniments
2 egg yolks, lightly beaten	

Grease a 2-quart ring mold with soft butter. Chill.

Preheat oven to 375° F.

Melt 1 tablespoon of the butter in a small frypan. Add the scallions and sauté until limp. Add the mushrooms and cook over low heat for about 10 minutes, stirring occasionally or until mushrooms are dry but not brown. Pour in the Madeira, raise the heat to medium and stir constantly to cook the wine away entirely. Remove from heat and set aside.

Melt remaining butter in a saucepan. Remove from heat and stir in the flour. Pour in the stock and stir with a whisk until blended. Return the pan to the heat and, stirring constantly, cook to a thick, smooth sauce.

Add a few tablespoons of the sauce to the egg yolks. Then, stirring rapidly, add egg mixture to sauce. Bring sauce to a boil. Remove from heat and season with salt, cayenne, paprika and lemon juice. Add the turkey, bread crumbs, and the mushroom mixture. Blend well and set aside to cool slightly.

In a large bowl beat the egg whites until stiff. Fold in the turkey mixture.

Pour into prepared mold, cover mold with foil and set in a pan of hot water.

Bake in preheated oven 35 to 40 minutes, or until firm.

Unmold and serve with CUMBERLAND SAUCE.

Serves 6 to 8.

Jellied Chicken with Almonds and Grapes

2 envelopes unflavored gelatin	2 cups diced cooked chicken or turkey
¼ cup dry white wine	½ cup finely chopped celery
1 cup chicken stock or broth	½ cup chopped almonds
1 cup mayonnaise	2 hard-cooked eggs, chopped
1 tablespoon lemon juice	½ pound seedless grapes
1 teaspoon salt	

Chill a 2-quart mold.

Sprinkle gelatin over wine and let stand about 5 minutes to soften. Heat stock to boiling. Remove from heat. Add softened gelatin and stir until dissolved. Refrigerate until mixture begins to thicken. Add mayonnaise and beat with a wire whisk until blended and smooth. Add remaining ingredients and blend until all are well coated.

Rinse chilled mold with cold water. Pour in the chicken mixture. Refrigerate until firm.

Unmold onto chilled platter and garnish with ripe green olives, carrot curls and sliced cucumbers.

Serves 8.

Turkey Pineapple Mold

1 8-ounce can crushed pineapple	1½ cups boiling water
2 envelopes unflavored gelatin	2 tablespoons lemon juice
3 chicken bouillon cubes	1½ cups diced cooked turkey
	¼ cup diced celery
	¼ cup chopped walnuts

Chill a 1-quart decorative mold.

Drain pineapple, reserving juice.

Put gelatin and bouillon cubes in container of electric blender. Add boiling water. Cover and blend at low speed for about 40 seconds, or until gelatin and bouillon are dissolved. Add lemon juice and reserved pineapple juice and blend. Transfer to a bowl and chill until thickened. Fold in turkey, drained crushed pineapple, celery and walnuts.

Rinse chilled mold with cold water. Pour in gelatin mixture. Chill until firm.

Unmold and garnish with slices of jellied cranberry sauce and watercress.

Serves 6 to 8.

TIMBALES

Chicken Timbales with Anchovy Sauce Andalouse

These timbales are as delicious as the most delicate soufflé; but unlike a soufflé, they are not temperamental. They can't fall and won't fail. Also unlike a soufflé which must be served as soon as it comes from the oven, they can wait until your guests are ready to come to the table.

4 tablespoons butter	⅓ cup milk
½ cup minced scallions	3 egg yolks
¼ cup dry white wine or vermouth	6 anchovy fillets, blotted dry
2 chicken breasts	3 egg whites
¾ cup crumbled firm white bread, crusts removed	SAUCE ANDALOUSE—see Sauces and Accompaniments

Generously butter six 1-cup timbale molds. Set aside.

Preheat oven to 350°F.

Heat the butter in a skillet over moderate heat. Add the scallions and sauté until limp. Add the wine and chicken breasts. Cover and cook over medium heat until chicken is tender—about 30 minutes. Set aside until cool.

Combine bread, milk, and egg yolks in medium bowl. Mix until smooth. Set aside.

Take chicken breasts from liquid. Remove skin and bones, and chop meat into small pieces. Add chicken and contents of the skillet and anchovies to bread mixture. Blend well.

Place mixture in container of electric blender and blend at medium speed to a smooth purée.

Beat egg whites until stiff enough to stand in soft peaks when beater is lifted from bowl. Gently fold chicken purée into beaten egg whites.

Spoon into prepared timbale molds. Place in a baking pan and pour in sufficient water to come halfway up sides of molds.

Place on lower rack of preheated oven and bake for 45 to 50 minutes until firm to the touch.

Let stand at room temperature for about 5 minutes, then turn out onto individual serving plates.

Spoon a little SAUCE ANDALOUSE over each when ready to serve. Serves 6.

FISH

Unlike almost all other fish dishes, hot fish and seafood molds can usually be prepared ahead. Again, unlike other fish dishes, they need not be eaten the minute they are cooked. They are, shall we say, "polite" and wait in their water bath for at least a half hour after they are ready to serve.

Cold fish and seafood mousses as well as aspics must, of course, be made ahead, which can make the cook's life easier.

Beyond these virtues molded fish and seafood are usually inexpensive and always superb.

HORS D'OEUVRES

Seafood Mold

1 pound boiled shrimp, shelled and deveined	½ pound butter at room temperature
1 tablespoon capers, well drained	2 tablespoons cognac or brandy
¼ small white onion	½ teaspoon salt

Finely mince shrimp, capers and onion. Combine with the butter and beat with a heavy wooden spoon until well blended and very smooth. Add the cognac or brandy and salt. Blend well.

Pack into a small (2-cup) mold. Chill.

Unmold and serve with unsalted crackers or as part of an antipasto or salad platter for a buffet supper.

VARIATION: You may use frozen shelled shrimp and deveined boiled shrimp. Just use as soon as they are completely thawed.

LOAVES

Curried Fish Loaf

3 tablespoons butter
2 teaspoons curry
  powder
2 tablespoons flour
1½ cups milk
1½ cups bread crumbs
1 pound fish fillets—
  flounder, codfish or
  haddock—preferably
  fresh, but frozen may
  be substituted if com-
  pletely thawed

5 egg whites
1 teaspoon salt
¼ teaspoon freshly
  ground pepper
MUSHROOM SAUCE OR
  TOMATO SAUCE—see
  Sauces and
  Accompaniments

Grease a 2-quart rectangular mold or loaf pan with soft butter. Chill.

Preheat oven to 425°F.

Melt the butter in a saucepan and stir in the curry powder. Cook, stirring a few seconds, then stir in the flour. When blended, slowly add 1 cup of the milk, stirring as it is added. Stir to a smooth thick sauce. Remove from heat. Cover the surface of sauce with plastic wrap and set aside at room temperature until cool.

Combine remaining milk and bread crumbs, and blend to a paste. Set aside.

Cut the fish into small pieces. Place half of the fish and half of the egg whites in container of electric blender. Blend at medium speed to a thick paste—about 1 minute. Transfer to a large mixing bowl. Blend remaining fish and egg whites in the same manner, and refrigerate.

When thoroughly chilled, combine fish mixture with cooled

sauce, and beat with a wooden spoon until light and smooth in texture. Fold in the milk and bread paste. Add salt and pepper.

Spoon into prepared mold and cover mold loosely with foil.

Bake in preheated oven for 45 to 50 minutes, or until firm. A knife inserted in center should come out clean.

Unmold and serve with MUSHROOM SAUCE or TOMATO SAUCE. Serves 6 to 8.

MOLDS

Creamy Codfish Mold with Tomato Horseradish Sauce

3 tablespoons butter	1 tablespoon horseradish
1 small white onion, peeled and finely minced	3–4 dashes Tabasco sauce
	3 egg whites
1 12-ounce can Gordon's Brand codfish cake mix	TOMATO HORSERADISH SAUCE —see Sauces and Accompaniments
3 egg yolks	

Grease a 1-quart melon or fish mold with oil and invert on paper toweling to drain. Set aside.

Preheat oven to 350°F.

Melt the butter in a large saucepan. Add the minced onion and sauté until limp. Remove pan from heat. Add the codfish and mash into the butter and onions with an old-fashioned potato masher, a fork or a heavy wooden spoon. Add egg yolks and continue to mash until no lumps remain and mixture is smooth. Stir in horseradish and Tabasco.

In a separate bowl beat egg whites until stiff. Fold in a little of the codfish mixture, then add to the rest of the codfish mixture and fold gently until no streaks of white remain.

Spoon into prepared mold. Place mold in a baking pan and pour in sufficient hot water to come halfway up sides of mold.

Place on middle rack of preheated oven and bake 45 to 50 minutes, or until firm.

Unmold and serve with TOMATO HORSERADISH SAUCE or sauce of your preference.

Serves 4.

Show-off Cold Fish Mold
(Super Easy)

1 13-ounce can
  madrilène
2 envelopes unflavored
  gelatin
2 6½- to 7-ounce cans
  salmon

½ cup milk
1 tablespoon horseradish
2 to 3 dashes Tabasco
  sauce
½ cup sour cream

Chill a 1- or 1½-quart decorative fish mold.

Pour 1 cup of the madrilène in top of a double boiler. Sprinkle 1 envelope of gelatin over surface. Let stand 2 or 3 minutes to soften. Place over simmering water and stir until gelatin is completely dissolved. Pour into a small (preferably metal) bowl and refrigerate until chilled and beginning to thicken. Stir occasionally to insure even consistency.

Rinse out chilled mold with cold water. Pour chilled madrilène into mold. Refrigerate until firm.

Place salmon in a large mixing bowl and mash smooth with an old-fashioned potato masher or a fork.

In a small bowl sprinkle remaining envelope of gelatin over milk. Let stand 2 or 3 minutes to soften.

Heat remaining madrilène to boiling. Pour in softened gelatin and stir until gelatin has dissolved. Pour mixture over mashed salmon, add horseradish and Tabasco sauce, and stir until blended. Stir in sour cream. Refrigerate until cool but not firm. Pour over madrilène-lined fish mold.

Place mold in a large pan and prop steady, if necessary, to keep from tilting. Refrigerate until set.

Unmold onto chilled platter.

Garnish with watercress, lemon wedges and ripe olives.

Serves 4 to 6.

Ring Mold of Flounder with Salmon

8 *fillets of flounder*	½ *cup butter at room*
(about 2 pounds)	*temperature*
¼ *cup lemon juice*	½ *cup flour*
Salt	*4 eggs*
1 *6½- or 7-ounce can*	2–3 *dashes Tabasco*
salmon	*sauce*
½ *cup clam juice*	1 *tablespoon horse-*
	radish

Grease a 1½-quart mold generously with butter.

Preheat oven to 350° F.

Line mold with fish fillets, narrow ends to center and over-hanging the outside and inside rims. Sprinkle with lemon juice and salt. Refrigerate until ready to use.

Drain salmon, place in a mixing bowl and mash until smooth.

In a large saucepan heat clam juice and half of the butter until butter melts and mixture comes to a full boil. Remove from heat and add flour all at once, stirring with a wooden spoon until mixture leaves the sides of the pan and forms a ball.

Transfer to a mixing bowl. Add eggs one at a time, beating well with electric beater or by hand with a heavy wooden spoon after each addition. Add salmon, Tabasco sauce and horseradish. Beat with electric beater for about 5 minutes at high speed, or by hand with a heavy wooden spoon, until mixture is light and smooth. Beat in half of remaining butter.

Fill fish-lined mold with salmon mixture. Fold ends of fillets, overlapping, over top. Spread remaining butter over surface.

Place mold in a baking pan and cover top loosely with a square of foil. Pour enough boiling water around mold to come to half-way up sides of mold.

Bake 45 minutes, or until firm.

Remove mold from water and let stand at room temperature for about 10 minutes.

Unmold onto serving platter. Let stand about 1 minute; then, holding mousse in place, tip platter slightly and pour off accumulated watery liquid.

Fill center with creamed carrots and onions or with mushrooms in cream sauce and serve at once.

Serves 6 to 8.

Norwegian Fiskepudding (Norwegian Fish Pudding)

Fish pudding is served in Norway at least once a week. And it's a versatile addition to our American cuisine. Served hot with SHRIMP SAUCE or LOBSTER SAUCE, it's a party dish. Served with a simple tomato sauce with creamed peas and celery or with melted butter, it's great family fare—easy to prepare and inexpensive. It's also good cold, sliced thinly and served as an appetizer with HORSERADISH MAYONNAISE and sour pickles, or thickly sliced and spread with mustard as a hearty sandwich filling.

It can be steamed on top of the stove or baked in the oven.

2 pounds fresh cod fillets without skin or 2 16-ounce packages frozen white fish fillets, thawed and skin removed	1½ cups light cream or 1¼ cup light cream and ¼ cup dry white wine 2 tablespoons cornstarch 2 teaspoons salt 1 cup heavy cream

Grease a 6-cup mold or casserole dish generously with a mixture of soft butter and corn or safflower oil.

With a sharp knife cut fish fillets into small pieces, discarding any bones.

Place about 3 tablespoons of the light cream or cream and wine mixture in container of electric blender. Add a few pieces of the fish and blend at high speed until smooth. Scrape mixture into large mixing bowl. Continue until all fish, light cream and wine are used. Stir in cornstarch and salt.

In a separate bowl beat heavy cream with a wire whisk until frothy but not stiff.

Gently fold cream, a little at a time, into fish mixture, beating well after each addition. (This slow, thorough addition of the cream and its proper incorporation is the secret of a smooth and light pudding.) When mixture seems fluffy, pour into prepared mold and smooth top.

Cover mold with its own cover or cover with a well-buttered sheet of foil, buttered side down. Use a sturdy rubber band to hold foil in place or tie down with butchers' string.

To steam, place mold on a rack or crumbled round of foil in a large pot; add sufficient hot water to cover bottom of pot by 2 inches. Simmer without boiling about 1 hour, or until a knife inserted in center comes out clean. Add additional water if necessary.

To bake, preheat oven to 350°F. Place mold in a 13" x 9" baking pan and add sufficient hot water to come ¾ up sides of mold. Bake about 1 hour, or until a knife inserted in center comes out clean.

To serve hot, unmold onto serving plate. Spoon some SHRIMP SAUCE or LOBSTER SAUCE over the surface. Pass additional sauce at the table.

To serve cold, cover mold and refrigerate pudding several hours until well chilled. Turn out onto serving plate and garnish with sprigs of parsley and lemon wedges. Serve desired cold sauce separately.

Serves 6.

Molded Deviled Sardines

2 3¾-ounce cans sardines	1 tablespoon lemon juice
1 tablespoon prepared mustard	¼ pound butter at room temperature
1 tablespoon horseradish	Salt
	Pepper

Mash sardines to a paste. Stir in mustard, horseradish and lemon juice. Add butter and blend well. Season with salt and pepper.

Pack into one or two ½- to 1-cup molds. Chill.

Unmold and serve with unsalted crackers.

Makes about 1 cup.

MOUSSES

Mousse de Poisson Amandine
(Fish Mousse with Almonds)

1 pound fish fillets—flounder, cod or haddock—preferably fresh, but frozen can be substituted if completely thawed	1 slice lemon, quartered
	½ teaspoon salt
	½ cup finely chopped almonds
1 tablespoon butter	½ cup fine dry bread crumbs
½ cup dry white wine or vermouth	½ cup light cream
1 thickly sliced onion, broken into rings	4 egg yolks
	4 egg whites

Generously grease a 2-quart fish or ring mold with soft butter. Refrigerate until ready to use.

Preheat oven to 350°F.

Place fish fillets in single layer in a long shallow baking pan. Dot with butter. Pour in wine and cover with onion rings and quartered lemon slice. Sprinkle with salt. Cover. Bake fish for about 20 minutes until firm and easily flaked when tested with a fork.

Flake the fish into a large mixing bowl. Strain and add the cooking liquid. Add almonds, bread crumbs, cream and egg yolks. Blend thoroughly.

Beat egg whites until stiff. Fold into fish mixture. Pour into prepared mold. Cover and seal with foil.

Place mold in a baking pan and pour in sufficient water to come ¾ up sides of mold.

Place on middle rack of preheated oven and bake for 1 hour, or until a knife inserted in center comes out clean.

Remove from oven and let stand about 5 minutes before un-molding onto hot serving platter.

Serves 4 to 6.

Halibut Mousse with Lobster Sauce

1 16-ounce package
  frozen fish fillets,
  thawed several hours
  at room temperature
  or overnight in the
  refrigerator
2 tablespoons butter
¼ cup dry white wine

½ teaspoon salt
¼ teaspoon pepper
⅛ teaspoon dried basil
3 egg yolks
1 cup sour cream
3 egg whites
LOBSTER SAUCE—see Sauces
  and Accompaniments

Generously grease a 1½-quart fish mold or other decorative mold with a mixture of mild oil and butter. Refrigerate until ready to use.

Preheat oven to 350°F.

Place thawed fillets, butter, wine, salt, pepper and basil in a skillet. Cover and simmer over low heat until fish is firm and flakes easily with a fork—about 10 minutes.

Flake fish into small pieces. Transfer entire contents of skillet to container of electric blender, add egg yolks and sour cream. Blend at high speed until mixture is smooth.

In a large mixing bowl beat egg whites until stiff. Slowly fold in fish mixture.

Pour into prepared mold.

Place in a baking dish and pour in sufficient water to come about halfway up sides of mold.

Place on middle rack of preheated oven and bake until firm—35 to 45 minutes.

Unmold onto serving platter and spoon some of the LOBSTER SAUCE over surface. Serve remaining sauce alongside entree.

Serves 4 to 6.

Mousse de Mer

1 cup bottled clam juice	2 envelopes unflavored
½ cup dry white wine	gelatin
1 clove garlic, peeled	3 tablespoons lemon
1 bay leaf	juice
8 ounces fish fillets	1 cup sour cream
8 ounces scallops	Paprika to season
1 pound shrimp	

Chill a 1½-quart ring mold.

Put clam juice, wine, garlic and bay leaf in a large skillet and bring to a boil. Add fish fillets, scallops and shrimp. Cover and simmer until shrimp turn pink—about 3 minutes. Remove shrimp with a slotted spoon and set aside. Cover and simmer until scallops are firm—about 2 additional minutes. Remove scallops and set aside. Let fillets continue to cook until flesh flakes easily when tested with a fork. Remove fillets. Strain cooking liquid, measure and reserve ½ cup plus 1 tablespoon. Pour this into a saucepan and heat to boiling.

In container of electric blender combine gelatin and lemon juice. Add boiling liquid and blend at high speed for 30 seconds. Break up and add fish fillets, scallops, sour cream and paprika. Blend at high speed for 20 seconds.

Rinse chilled mold with cold water. Pour in mousse mixture. Chill until firm.

Shell and devein shrimp. Chill. When ready to serve, unmold jellied ring onto a large platter and fill center with mayonnaise. Surround with chilled shrimp, black olives, tomato wedges and wedges of hard-cooked eggs.

Serves 4 to 6.

Mousse of Shrimp with Fillet of Sole

Definitely a company dish that looks and tastes like haute cuisine but, with the help of an electric blender, is both quick and easy to prepare.

In this recipe I have filled the center of the mousse with creamed peas and tiny white onions in CREAMY TOMATO SAUCE, but any creamed vegetables can be substituted. What you choose, however, should have color as the mousse is creamy white and needs contrast. If you prefer not to fill the center, simply make half of the CREAMY TOMATO SAUCE and spoon over and around mousse.

1 pound raw shrimp	2 tablespoons brandy
8 sole fillets (about 2¼ pounds)	2 tablespoons dry sherry
¼ cup lemon juice	Butter at room temperature
Salt	PEAS AND ONIONS IN TOMATO
2 egg whites	SAUCE—see Sauces and
1 cup heavy cream	Accompaniments
1 teaspoon salt	CREAMY TOMATO SAUCE—
1 teaspoon tomato paste	see Sauces and Accompaniments

Generously grease a 1½-quart ring mold with butter and refrigerate until ready to use.

Shell and devein shrimp. Chop coarsely. Refrigerate, covered, until ready to use.

Rinse sole fillets with cold running water and blot dry with paper toweling. Brush each fillet with lemon juice.

Line greased mold with fish fillets, dark side up and narrow ends to center. Allow fillets to overhang the outside and inside rims. Sprinkle with salt.

Place egg whites, cream, salt, tomato paste, brandy, sherry and chopped shrimp in electric blender. Cover and blend at high speed for about 2 minutes, or until mixture is smooth. Spoon into fillet-lined mold. Fold ends of fillets overlapping on top. Spread with soft butter.

(This can be prepared several hours ahead and refrigerated until time to bake.)

Preheat oven to 350°F.

Place mold in a baking pan and cover top loosely with a square of foil. Pour enough boiling water around mold to come halfway up sides of mold.

Bake 30 minutes, or until just firm.

To unmold, use a spatula to loosen edges of ring and carefully pour off any liquid. (You can add this to the CREAMY TOMATO SAUCE.) Invert over heated platter and lift off mold.

Fill center of mousse with PEAS AND ONIONS IN TOMATO SAUCE. Garnish with sautéed mushrooms and sprigs of watercress.

Serves 6.

Shrimp and Avocado Mousse

½ pound large shrimp
2 tablespoons cider vinegar
3 tablespoons corn or safflower oil
¾ teaspoon salt
¼ teaspoon freshly ground black pepper
¼ teaspoon dry mustard
1 clove garlic
3 envelopes unflavored gelatin

1 cup cold water
2 cups tomato juice
4 large avocados—or sufficient to make 4 cups mashed avocado
¼ cup strained lemon juice
¼ cup dry white wine
3–4 dashes Tabasco sauce
1 teaspoon salt

Fill a large pot with water and bring to a full boil. Add shrimp. Let water return to boil. Cook shrimp 1 to 2 minutes, or until firm and pink. Don't overcook. Drain, cool slightly, peel and devein. Split each shrimp down the back without separating the halves. Press each out flat like a butterfly. Place in nonmetal bowl.

Combine vinegar, oil, salt, pepper and mustard. Pour over shrimp. Add garlic. Cover and refrigerate several hours.

To prepare aspic:

Soften 2 envelopes of the gelatin in ½ cup of cold water. Heat tomato juice to steamy hot, but do not allow to boil. Stir in softened gelatin. Refrigerate until well chilled and thickened.

To prepare mold:

Place chilled mold in a large bowl of ice. Add a small amount of the chilled aspic, then turn the mold so that the jelly runs around the sides and covers the bottom. Push down into ice to chill quickly. When almost firm repeat 3 or 4 times. When the mold is completely lined with a thick layer of gelatin, refrigerate until it is almost set but feels "sticky" to the finger. Return reserved aspic to refrigerator.

Drain shrimp and pat dry. Dip each in the chilled-but-still-liquid reserved aspic and arrange in a pattern on aspic layer in mold. Chill until firm, then pour remaining aspic over surface. Refrigerate again until firm.

Soften third envelope of gelatin in the remaining ½ cup water in top of double boiler.

Peel avocados, remove pits and mash until smooth.

Add lemon juice, wine, Tabasco sauce and salt to softened gelatin, and stir over simmering water until gelatin is completely dissolved. Add to mashed avocado and blend well. Spoon over firm shrimp and tomato aspic. Chill until avocado mixture is also firm.

Unmold onto serving dish and garnish with sliced cucumbers and tomato wedges.

Serve with mayonnaise.

Serves 6 to 8.

Cold Tunafish Mousse

2 envelopes unflavored gelatin	¼ cup mayonnaise
½ cup cold water	1 tablespoon tomato paste
¾ cup clear, fat-free chicken stock	1 cup sour cream
1 7-ounce can tuna fish	1 teaspoon horseradish
¼ cup finely chopped celery	Salt
	Pepper

Grease a 1½-quart mold (a decorative fish mold if you have one) with oil. Invert onto paper toweling to drain off excess oil. Set aside.

Sprinkle gelatin over cold water and let stand at room temperature to soften.

Heat chicken stock to boiling. Stir in softened gelatin and

stir over low heat until completely dissolved. Cool to room temperature.

Place tuna fish in a large mixing bowl and mash with a heavy wooden spoon until smooth. Add cooled stock and blend well. Stir in chopped celery, mayonnaise, tomato paste, sour cream and horseradish. Season with salt and pepper. Spoon into prepared mold and refrigerate several hours until firm.

Set mold in a pan of hot water for a moment. Loosen sides with a knife. Unmold onto a chilled platter. Garnish with pimento strips, black olives and lemon wedges.

Serve with a bowl of mayonnaise or tartar sauce.

Serves 4 to 6.

TIMBALES

Chinese-style Shrimp Timbales

2 cups water	1 teaspoon Chinese rice
1 clove garlic, peeled	wine or sherry
½ pound raw shrimp	1 teaspoon soy sauce
6 eggs	½ teaspoon finely
1 tablespoon corn or	chopped ginger or
safflower oil	powdered ginger

Grease 6 individual timbale molds or custard cups with mild oil. Invert on paper toweling to drain off excess oil.

Place water and garlic in a saucepan and bring to a full boil. Add shrimp and cook only until shells turn pink—about 1 minute. Remove shrimp from water with a slotted spoon and allow to cool slightly. Let water continue to boil while you shell, devein, and coarsely chop shrimp.

Reserve ⅓ cup of the cooking water. Cool. Discard remaining water and garlic.

In a mixing bowl with a wire whisk or in an electric blender beat eggs with cooled shrimp water, oil, rice wine or sherry and soy sauce until well blended. Add shrimp and ginger.

Pour mixture into prepared timbale molds or custard cups.

Place each mold on a crumbled round of foil in a large pot. Pour in sufficient hot water to cover bottom of pot by 2 inches. Bring to a boil. Reduce heat so that water simmers. Cover the pot and let timbales steam until firm. A silver knife inserted in center should come out clean. Add additional hot water if needed.

Unmold timbales onto individual serving plates. Garnish with parsley.

Serve hot or at room temperature.

Serves 6.

EGGS AND CHEESE

HORS D'OEUVRES

Frozen Cheese Mousse

½ pound Roquefort or
  blue cheese
1 cup plus 2 tablespoons
  heavy cream

2 egg whites
Tabasco sauce

Chill a 1-quart mold.

Crumble cheese. Add 2 tablespoons heavy cream and mash until smooth and pliable. Beat the egg whites until stiff. In a separate bowl beat the remaining 1 cup of cream until stiff. Fold the cheese mixture into the egg whites, then fold in the whipped cream. Season with a dash of Tabasco.

Spoon into chilled mold and freeze.

To serve, unmold on a bed of crushed ice and serve with piping hot, unsalted crackers.

Makes about 2 cups.

Egg and Caviar Mousse

This is an excellent way to "extend" a small jar of caviar.

1 dozen hard-cooked
  eggs
4 tablespoons butter
4 ounces black or red
  caviar
2 tablespoons cognac or
  brandy, or 3 table-
  spoons strained lemon
  juice

2–3 dashes Tabasco
  sauce
½ to ¾ cup onion,
  minced

Generously butter a small (1- to 2-cup) mold with soft butter. Chill.

Chop whites of hard cooked eggs. Set aside.

In a large mixing bowl combine hard-cooked egg yolks, butter, half of the caviar and the cognac, brandy or lemon juice and Tabasco sauce. Mash until smooth and pack into chilled mold. Chill several hours.

Unmold onto a large serving plate.

Combine remaining caviar, chopped egg whites and onion. Spoon around mousse. Surround with unsalted crackers. Provide hors d'oeuvre knives (or butter knives) and let guests help themselves—*i.e.*, spread a cracker with mousse and top with caviar, minced onion and chopped hard-cooked egg white mixture.

NOTE: Though appetites vary and everyone seems to help themselves generously to this hors d'oeuvre, I think you'll find this recipe sufficient to satisfy 6 to 8 guests.

Fromage à la Crème

1 6-ounce package cream cheese	1 pint cream-style cottage cheese
3 ounces blue or Roquefort cheese	1 cup sour cream
	2 tablespoons finely minced chives

Bring all cheeses to room temperature. Cream together the cream cheese, blue or Roquefort cheese and cottage cheese until totally free of lumps and very smooth. Use an old-fashioned potato masher or a heavy wooden spoon.

Stir in the sour cream and chives. Blend well. Place mixture in a colander to drain overnight in the refrigerator. Next day pack into a 1-quart round-bottomed mold which has first been lined with cheesecloth. Refrigerate for several hours.

Unmold onto a chilled serving platter.

Serves 8 to 10 as a cocktail hors d'oeuvre.

MOLDS

Cottage Cheese Ring

3 cups cream-style cottage cheese	1 teaspoon seasoned salt
2–3 tablespoons sour cream	1–2 teaspoons celery seed (optional)
	Paprika

Lightly grease a 1-quart ring mold with mayonnaise.

Mix cottage cheese with sour cream and seasoned salt and celery seed. Pack into prepared mold. Chill.

Unmold onto a large round platter. Sprinkle generously with paprika.

You can fill this mold in so many different ways. Combinations I find attractive are:

Melon balls (just thawed frozen ones may be substituted for fresh) combined with orange and grapefruit sections. Mix them with just enough French dressing for flavor.

Fresh sliced peaches or strawberries, or a combination of both, lightly sugared and mixed with chopped fresh mint leaves.

Canned artichoke hearts (drained and halved) and pitted black olives mixed with hearts of lettuce.

Jumbo boiled shrimp (peeled and deveined) mixed with pink grapefruit sections, moistened with garlicky Italian dressing.

Any combination of canned or fresh fruit, spiked with rum or cognac and lightly sweetened with sugar.

A mixed green salad put together with vinaigrette dressing spiked with paprika.

Quick and Easy Tomato Cheese Mold

1 can condensed cream
   of tomato soup
1 cup cheddar cheese,
   crumbled or cut into
   cubes
5 egg yolks
⅛ teaspoon salt

3–4 dashes Tabasco sauce
8–10 pimento stuffed
   olives, chopped
5 egg whites
Butter and bread crumbs
   for mold

Grease a 2-quart ring mold lightly with butter. Sprinkle with bread crumbs. Rotate mold to distribute crumbs evenly. Invert and shake out excess crumbs.

Preheat oven to 325°F.

Heat soup in top of double boiler to steamy hot. Add cheese and cook, stirring constantly, over simmering water until cheese has melted. Remove from heat and cool slightly.

Beat egg yolks in a large mixing bowl until frothy. Add about ¼ cup of the soup mixture and beat rapidly with a wire whisk until blended. Stir in remaining soup and cheese mixture, salt, Tabasco and chopped olives. Blend well. Cool to room temperature.

Beat egg whites until stiff. Fold into soup mixture. Pour into prepared mold. Place mold in a baking pan and pour in sufficient water to come ¾ up sides of mold.

Place on middle rack of preheated oven and bake 45 to 50 minutes, or until firm.

Remove from oven and let stand at room temperature about 5 minutes.

Unmold onto hot serving platter.

Fill center with buttered lima beans or any desired vegetable. Serves 4 to 6.

Oeufs Moulés
(Molded Eggs)

OEUFS MOULÉS are the "answer" way to serve eggs for a casual buffet party, as they can be prepared ahead of time, then cooked quickly after guests arrive.

Butter any small decorative molds (custard cups, Timbale molds, etc.) that are large enough to hold 1 egg—approximately ⅓ cup. Sprinkle with salt. Chill.

Preheat oven to 375°F.

Break the eggs into the chilled molds. Dot with slivers of butter. Cover and seal each mold with foil, and set molds in a baking pan. Pour in sufficient water to come halfway up sides of molds.

Bake in preheated oven 6 to 8 minutes, or until eggs are firm. Let stand at room temperature briefly before unmolding.

Unmold and serve "à la crème"—topped with a teaspoon of heavy cream and sprinkled with paprika; Portugaise—topped with one or two anchovies; Italian—topped with tomato sauce; or American—served with crisp bacon and toast points.

Rarebit Ring

2 *tablespoons butter*	1 *cup grated sharp*
3 *egg yolks*	*cheddar cheese*
½ *cup heavy cream*	½ *cup ale*
½ *teaspoon salt*	3 *egg whites*
½ *teaspoon dry*	
mustard	

Grease a 1½- or 2-quart ring mold generously with soft butter.

Preheat oven to 350°F.

Melt butter. Cool.

Beat egg yolks until frothy. Add cream, salt, mustard, cheese, ale and cooled melted butter. Beat until well blended.

Beat egg whites until stiff. Fold in yolk mixture. Pour into prepared mold.

Place mold in a baking pan and pour in sufficient hot water to come halfway up sides of mold.

Bake for 25 to 30 minutes, or until firm.

Unmold and serve with crisp cooked bacon or spicy little link sausages, crusty bread and cold beer.

Serves 4.

TIMBALES

Brunch Timbales

Served with little link sausages (which you can cook ahead and reheat just before serving) and broiled apple slices sprinkled with brown sugar and dotted with butter, they make a delicious but easy to prepare brunch menu.

1½ cups light cream or ¾ cup light cream and ¾ cup chicken stock
4 eggs
1 tablespoon prepared mustard
Dash Tabasco sauce
1 tablespoon tomato catsup or chili sauce
1 tablespoon horseradish
½ teaspoon salt
¼ teaspoon cayenne

Grease 4 timbale molds with soft butter. Chill.

Preheat oven to 350°F.

Heat cream or cream and stock until warm.

Beat eggs until blended. Stir in remaining ingredients. Warm cream (or cream and stock) and blend well with egg mixture.

Pour into prepared molds. Place in a baking pan and pour in sufficient hot water to come halfway up sides of molds.

Bake in preheated oven until firm—about 20 minutes.

Let stand 2 or 3 minutes before unmolding.

Serves 4.

NOTE: The timbale mixture can be prepared ahead of time and poured into molds when you are ready to bake.

Cheese Timbales

Cheese timbales are never fail and versatile. They are light, yet filling and delicious. They may be served as a first course for a company dinner or as an excellent addition to a vegetable luncheon plate. Top them with any number of sauces, serve plain or garnish with a crisscross of pimento strips or anchovy fillets.

4 eggs
1½ cups chicken stock, canned or homemade and free of all fat
½ cup heavy cream
2 tablespoons grated sharp cheddar, Swiss or mild American cheese
½ teaspoon salt
MUSHROOM SAUCE or CREAMY TOMATO SAUCE— see Sauces and Accompaniments

Generously grease 4 individual molds or custard cups. Refrigerate until ready to use.

Preheat oven to 350° F.

Beat eggs in a large mixing bowl until frothy. Add remaining ingredients (except sauce) and beat with a wire whisk until thoroughly blended. Pour into prepared molds or custard cups.

Set the molds on a rack in a baking pan and pour in sufficient hot water to come ¾ up sides of molds.

Place on center rack in preheated oven and bake 20 to 25 minutes, or until firm.

Unmold and serve with CREAMY TOMATO SAUCE, MUSHROOM SAUCE or any creamed vegetable.

Serves 4.

Cheddar Cheese Mold

This is a low calorie, rich tasting timbale. Dieters will love you for this one.

¾ *cup milk*
½ *cup cottage cheese*
2 *egg yolks*
2 *tablespoons grated or*
  crumbled sharp
  cheddar cheese

Dash Tabasco sauce
½ *teaspoon salt*

Generously grease four ½-cup molds or custard cups. Refrigerate until ready to use.

Preheat oven to 350°F.

Heat milk to steamy hot. Pour into container of electric blender. Add cottage cheese and blend at high speed for a few seconds. Add remaining ingredients and blend at medium speed until mixture is smooth.

Pour into greased molds.

Place molds in a baking pan and add sufficient water to come ¾ up sides of molds.

Place on middle rack of preheated oven and bake 20 to 25 minutes, or until firm.

Unmold onto heated serving plates.

Serves 4.

POTATOES,
RICE & PASTA

More often than not, our main dishes are accompanied by potatoes, rice or pasta, in one form or another. All too frequently, however, they are indifferently prepared and unimaginatively served. With a mold and a little effort, you can lift them out of their commonplace role as the "starchy part of the meal" and transform them into true delicacies.

MOLDS

Macaroni Ring with Ham and Cheese

8 ounces elbow
  macaroni
4 large eggs
1 cup heavy cream
½ cup grated Swiss
  cheese

⅓ to ¾ cup finely
  chopped lean baked
  ham
Salt
Pepper

Generously grease a 2-quart ring mold with butter. Chill.
  Preheat oven to 375°F.
  Cook macaroni according to package directions. Drain.
  Beat the eggs in a mixing bowl until frothy. Add cream and
cheese. Blend, then add the macaroni and ham. Season with salt
and pepper. Pour into prepared mold. Set mold in a baking dish
and pour in sufficient water to come halfway up sides of mold.
  Bake for 25 to 30 minutes, or until firm.
  Unmold and serve with tomato or cheese sauce, or fill center
with steamed carrots and peas, or any desired vegetable.
  Serves 4 to 6.

Classic Noodle Ring

8 ounces noodles
2 tablespoons butter at
  room temperature

1 tablespoon heavy
  cream
1 tablespoon grated
  Parmesan cheese

Generously grease a 1-quart ring mold with butter.
  Preheat oven to 200°F.

Cook noodles according to package directions. Drain into a colander, then return to cooking pot while it is still hot. Add the butter, cream and Parmesan cheese. Toss until cheese and butter are melted.

Turn into prepared ring mold. Cover and seal mold with foil. Set the mold in a baking pan and pour in sufficient boiling water to come halfway up sides of mold. Set in preheated oven until ready to use—up to 30 minutes.

Unmold and fill center with creamed seafood or chicken, Italian meatballs in tomato sauce, or any other sauced, tasty mixture.

Serves 4 to 6.

Noodle Ring with Boursin Cheese

You can fill the center of this ring mold with creamy mixed vegetables, chicken or seafood in cream sauce, Italian tomato sauce with meatballs or just about any other delicious mixture.

8 ounces flat noodles
1 tablespoon butter at
   room temperature
1 cup light cream

4 eggs
1 package Boursin
   cheese with herbs
½ teaspoon salt

Generously butter a 1-quart ring mold. Set aside.

Preheat oven to 325°F.

Cook noodles according to package directions. Drain into a colander, then return to the cooking pot while it is still hot. Add butter and fork stir until butter is melted.

Heat cream to steamy hot.

Beat eggs in medium bowl until blended. Add crumbled cheese and salt. Pour in hot cream. Add noodles and toss lightly until ingredients are blended. Pour into prepared mold.

Place mold in a baking pan and pour in enough hot water to come ¾ up sides of mold.

Place on middle rack of preheated oven and bake for 1 hour, or until firm.

Unmold onto serving platter.

Serves 4 to 6.

Polenta Ring

1 cup yellow cornmeal	1 tablespoon grated
1 teaspoon salt	Parmesan cheese
4 cups water at room	
temperature	

Grease a 1-quart ring mold generously with soft butter. Chill. Preheat oven to 200°F.

Combine cornmeal with salt in a mixing bowl. Add 2 cups of the water and stir until blended.

Bring remaining water to a boil in top half of double boiler over direct heat. Stir in cornmeal mixture. Bring to a full boil, stirring constantly. Place over simmering water, and cook covered, stirring occasionally until thick—about 30 minutes. Stir in cheese.

Pour mixture into prepared mold.

Place mold in a baking pan and pour in sufficient hot water to come ¾ up sides of mold. Place in preheated oven until ready to unmold and serve—up to 30 minutes.

Fill center as desired. My first choice is Italian meatballs in tomato sauce, but for a quick and easy supper dish I've also used canned chili with beans, topped with grated Jack (or sharp cheddar) cheese and shredded lettuce. My guests thought it "very special."

Molded Potatoes à la Russe

This is an all-time favorite dish of my friends Bob and Mary Haggerty. They like to come over for breakfast early on Sunday mornings. The menu is corned beef hash with poached eggs, MOLDED POTATOES À LA RUSSE, grilled tomato slices and broiled peaches. We end the meal with plenty of strong hot coffee and my baker's best Danish.

4 large baking potatoes	Salt
4 tablespoons butter, cut	½ cup sour cream
into slivers	

Generously butter a 1½-quart round bottomed mold with soft butter. Chill.

Preheat oven to 350°F.

Boil whole potatoes in sufficient water to cover by 1 inch until soft enough to pierce easily with a small sharp knife. Don't overcook potatoes or they will crumble when sliced. Drain and cool. Peel and cut into thin slices.

Line the prepared mold completely with potato slices, letting them overlap slightly. Dot with slivers of butter and sprinkle lightly with salt. Spread about 2 tablespoons of sour cream over the potatoes. Repeat until all potatoes are used, ending with potatoes and butter slivers.

Bake for 30 to 45 minutes, or until surface of potatoes is flecked with brown. Unmold and garnish with watercress.

Serves 6 to 8.

Potatoes Anna

A classic recipe—an elegant and beautiful way to serve potatoes.

6 *large all-purpose potatoes*	*Salt*
	¼ *pound butter at room temperature*

Generously grease a 1-quart mold.

Preheat oven to 425°F.

Peel the potatoes and slice them very thinly into ovals of as nearly the same size as possible. Drop potatoes into a large pan of cold water as soon as they are sliced.

Let stand about 30 minutes, then drain and blot each slice thoroughly dry.

Arrange a layer of potato slices flat on the bottom of the mold and up the sides. Sprinkle lightly with salt and dot with soft butter. Repeat, covering mold completely. Continue layering until all slices are used and mold is full. Spread top with butter.

Place in preheated oven and bake for 40 to 45 minutes, or until potatoes are soft in center. Test with a small kitchen knife.

Invert mold and turn potatoes out onto a warm platter or plate in molded form—golden brown all over.

Serves 6.

Basic Rice Ring

Cold leftover or just-cooked white or brown rice can be pressed into a ring to serve as a border for any sauced food, such as creamed ham, curried seafood, vegetables in sour cream, beef in chili, chicken in Italian tomato sauce, jambalaya, etc.

3 cups cooked rice	*Pepper*
Salt	*2 tablespoons butter*

Generously grease a 1-quart ring mold.

Preheat oven to 350°F.

Season 3 cups cooked rice with salt and pepper to taste and pack into mold.

Melt butter and pour over surface.

Set the mold in a pan of hot water and place in a preheated oven. Bake 20 to 30 minutes.

Loosen the edges and invert the contents of the mold onto a heated platter.

Fill the center as desired and serve at once.

Serves 4 to 6.

Brown Rice Ring with Vegetables

The vegetables can be prepared early and reheated. The mold of rice can be covered and set into a pan of hot water. So it only takes a moment to assemble this attractive and delicious dish. If the artichoke hearts are too large, cut them in half; and if small mushrooms are not available, use thinly sliced mushrooms. The rice is especially good if cooked in chicken stock.

3 cups cooked brown
  rice
12 to 14 small white
  onions, peeled
¾ cup chicken stock,
  canned or homemade
1 teaspoon sugar
4 tablespoons butter

1 3-ounce can whole
  "button" mushrooms
2 teaspoons Madeira or
  sherry
8 to 10 artichoke hearts,
  canned or frozen
  (If frozen artichokes
  are used, defrost and
  drain.)

Generously butter a 1½-quart ring mold and gently pack the rice into it. Cover and set in a pan of hot water.

Put the onions into a small pot with ½ cup of the stock, cover and cook until tender. Drain. Return onions to pan, sprinkle with sugar, add 1 tablespoon butter, and stir until sugar has dissolved.

Melt the remaining butter in a skillet, add mushrooms and Madeira or sherry. Toss and cook over a high heat 2 or 3 minutes. Add onions and artichoke hearts. Lower the heat and add the remaining ¼ cup of stock. Cook, stirring often, for 5 to 10 minutes.

Unmold the rice ring onto a hot platter, and spoon the onions, mushrooms and artichokes into the center. Garnish with finely chopped parsley.

Serves 6.

Green and Gold Rice Ring

This very colorful and quick to make recipe was developed by the home economist of The Osterizer Company.

1 medium onion, peeled
  and chopped
2 cups coarsely chopped
  carrots
1 small green pepper,
  seeded, white section
  removed and coarsely
  chopped
1 4-ounce can pimentos

1 10-ounce can beef
  consomme
¼ cup water
½ teaspoon salt
¼ pound butter at room
  temperature
2 cups quick-cooking
  rice

Generously butter a 1½-quart ring mold.

Place first seven ingredients in container of electric blender, cover and blend until vegetables are finely chopped. Don't overblend—vegetables should be in uniform pieces of about ¼ inch. Empty into a medium saucepan. Add butter. Bring to a full boil, add rice and return to boil.

Cover saucepan, remove from heat and let stand about 5 minutes. Pack firmly into prepared mold. Either unmold immediately or place in a pan of hot water until ready to serve. However, it can be held this way no longer than 15 minutes. Serves 6.

Rice Pilaf Ring

This molded rice ring is perfect for curried chicken or seafood. The usual curry accompaniments are in the rice so that the only side dish needed is a small bowl of chutney.

1 teaspoon oil	2 tablespoons butter
3 cups water	⅓ cup chopped almonds
1 teaspoon salt	1 teaspoon finely
1½ cups natural brown	chopped, preserved
rice	(bottled in syrup)
⅓ cup currants or raisins	ginger, blotted dry
¼ cup Madeira	1 tablespoon soy sauce

Generously butter a 1-quart ring mold.

Preheat oven to 200°F.

Combine oil, water and salt. Bring to boil. Slowly add rice so that water continues to boil. Skim surface of water, removing all brown foam. Lower heat and simmer until rice is tender—about 30 minutes. Drain into a colander. Place colander over, not in, simmering water until rice is thoroughly dry. (Rice may be cooked ahead, covered and refrigerated until ready to proceed; or 3 to 3½ cups cold leftover rice may be substituted.)

Soak currants or raisins in Madeira for 30 minutes. Drain.

Melt butter in a large skillet. Add cooked rice and stir with fork. Stir in raisins or currants, almonds, chopped ginger and soy sauce. Remove from heat and transfer to buttered mold. Pack down firmly.

Place mold in preheated oven for 25 to 30 minutes.

Unmold. Fill center with very hot shrimp curry (or any creamed seafood or chicken), and serve at once.

Serves 6 to 8.

NOTE: The ring may be prepared one or even two days ahead. Store, covered, in refrigerator. To reheat, bring to room temperature, then place ring in a roasting pan and add water to a depth of about 2 inches. Place in a preheated 375°F. oven for about 15 minutes. Unmold onto heated platter.

TIMBALES

Potato Timbales with Garlic

These potato timbales are especially good with baked fish or sautéed shad roe. I also like them with roasted or braised lamb accompanied with mint jelly. If you like a garlicky taste—and most people do—you'll especially enjoy potatoes prepared in this manner.

5 or 6 cloves garlic
4 tablespoons butter
2 tablespoons flour
1 cup milk at room
    temperature
¼ teaspoon salt

1 tablespoon grated
    Parmesan cheese
2 pounds baking
    potatoes (about 3 large
    potatoes)
4 large eggs, separated

Grease 8 timbale molds generously with soft butter. Chill.

Preheat oven to 350°F.

Peel and coarsely chop garlic. Melt the butter in a saucepan. Add the garlic. Cover and cook over low heat until garlic is tender. Stir occasionally.

Stir in the flour. Remove pan from heat and slowly add the milk, stirring as it is added. Blend in salt and grated cheese.

Pour contents of pan into container of electric blender and blend to a purée (or force through a sieve). Pour mixture back into the saucepan. Cover surface of mixture with plastic wrap and set aside.

Cover potatoes with water and boil until tender enough to be pierced easily by a small sharp knife. Drain and peel while hot. Place in a large mixing bowl and mash until smooth.

Reheat the garlic sauce and add to the mashed potatoes a little at a time. Beat with a wooden spoon until light and fluffy.

Add the egg yolks one at a time, beating well after each addition.

Whip the egg whites until stiff. Whip in about ¼ of the potato mixture, then fold in remaining mixture.

Pour into prepared molds. Set molds in a baking pan and pour in sufficient water to come halfway up sides of molds.

Bake in preheated oven for about 30 minutes, or until firm.

Unmold and serve very hot.

Serves 8.

Rice Timbales with Swiss Cheese

This makes an inexpensive but extraordinarily good luncheon entree. Serve with a really good mixed green salad and hot rolls. Follow with an "easy to put together" dessert of ice cream and pound cake (laced with a bit of cognac) and freshly brewed coffee.

4 cups milk	*1 cup grated Swiss*
½ cup long grain rice	*cheese*
3 tablespoons butter	*1 teaspoon salt*
2 tablespoons flour	*4 eggs, separated*

Generously grease 6 timbale molds with soft butter. Chill.

Preheat oven to 350°F.

In a saucepan heat 1 cup of milk. Add the rice. Cover and cook over low heat until rice is tender and milk has been absorbed. Set aside.

Melt the butter in a large saucepan and stir in the flour. When blended, slowly add the remaining milk, stirring constantly. Add the grated cheese and salt. Cook, stirring, to a smooth thick sauce. Cool slightly, then add the egg yolks one at a time, beating well after each addition. Stir in the rice.

Beat the egg whites until stiff. Beat a small amount into the sauce rice mixture, then fold mixture into remaining whites.

Pour into prepared molds. Set molds in a baking pan and pour in sufficient hot water to come halfway up sides of molds.

Bake in preheated oven for 20 to 25 minutes, or until firm.

Unmold and serve very hot.
Makes 6 small servings.

Chinese Pork and Rice Timbales

Try these with chicken chow mein or chop suey. Add Chinese
egg rolls, and dinner is served.

2 tablespoons butter
1 cup diced, cooked lean
  pork
1 4-ounce can chopped
  mushrooms, well
  drained
¼ cup chopped onion
1½ cups quick cooking
  rice
1¼ cups water

¼ cup sherry (or sub-
  stitute water)
1 teaspoon soy sauce
Dash pepper
½ cup well-drained,
  canned water chest-
  nuts, chopped
3 eggs, well beaten
MUSTARD SAUCE—see
  Sauces and
  Accompaniments

Generously grease 6 timbale molds or custard cups.

Melt butter in a large saucepan. Add pork, mushrooms and
onion. Cook, stirring, until onion is limp. Add rice, water, sherry,
soy sauce, pepper and water chestnuts. Mix to moisten all rice.
Bring quickly to a boil. Cover, remove from heat and let stand
5 minutes. Add eggs and stir to blend thoroughly.

Pack firmly into buttered timbales or custard cups. Place each
on a rack, or on crumpled rounds of foil, in a large, heavy pot.
Pour in sufficient water to cover bottom of pot by about 2 inches.
Cover pot and place over low heat so that water simmers gently.
Let molds steam for 15 to 20 minutes.

Remove molds from pot and invert onto serving platter. Let
stand 1 minute before removing molds.

Serve with MUSTARD SAUCE.

Makes 6 small servings.

Tomato Rice Timbales

3 quarts water	1 tablespoon finely
1 teaspoon salt	minced onion
1 teaspoon mild oil	1 8-ounce can stewed
1½ cups long grain rice	tomatoes
2 tablespoons grated	2 tablespoons dry white
Parmesan cheese	wine
4 tablespoons butter at	1 teaspoon tomato paste
room temperature	¼ teaspoon salt

Grease six 1-cup timbale molds or custard cups with soft butter.

Preheat oven to 350° F.

In a large saucepan bring the water to a complete boil. Add salt and oil, then slowly add rice so that water continues to boil. Lower heat and simmer until rice is just tender—about 20 minutes. Drain into a colander. Place colander over a pan of simmering water and steam until completely dry. Transfer to a large mixing bowl. Using a fork, stir in cheese and 2 tablespoons of butter.

Melt remaining butter in a saucepan, add minced onion and sauté until limp. Add stewed tomatoes and wine. Stir in tomato paste and salt. Simmer, stirring often, until mixture is very thick and almost dry.

Add tomato mixture to rice and gently stir with a fork until ingredients are well blended.

Pack the rice solidly into prepared molds. Cover and seal each mold with foil. Place molds in a large baking pan and pour in sufficient hot water to come halfway up sides of molds.

Place on middle rack of preheated oven and bake 15 to 20 minutes or until very hot.

Unmold onto serving platter or individual serving plates.

Serves 6.

HOT VEGETABLES

Molded vegetables offer even the novice cook an opportunity to transform inexpensive ingredients into delicious and satisfying accompaniments to main dishes. With the high cost of meat and poultry they can often serve as the main course as well. The substitution of SPINACH TIMBALES with a cheese sauce, for example, or a tomato ring filled with creamed peas or lima beans can often be the solution to overworked budgets and overworked cooks.

MOLDS

Broccoli Walnut Ring Mold

1 10-ounce package
frozen chopped
broccoli
1 clove garlic
(optional)
4 tablespoons butter
1 tablespoon minced
onion
3 tablespoons flour

½ cup chicken stock or
milk
½ cup milk or light
cream
3 egg yolks
½ cup chopped walnuts
1 or 2 drops green food
coloring (optional)
3 egg whites

Grease a 1½-quart ring mold with soft butter. Chill.

Preheat oven to 350°F.

Cook broccoli according to package directions, adding garlic to cooking water. Drain. Discard garlic and mince broccoli.

Melt butter in a saucepan. Sauté onion until limp, then stir in flour. When blended, slowly add stock and milk or cream, stirring constantly. Cook, stirring, to a smooth thick sauce. Remove from heat and cool slightly. Stir in egg yolks, broccoli and walnuts. Blend. If desired, add 1 or 2 drops of green food coloring.

Beat the egg whites until stiff. Fold in broccoli mixture.

Pour into prepared mold. Place in a baking dish and pour in sufficient hot water to come halfway up sides of mold.

Bake for 30 to 35 minutes, or until firm. Let stand about 5 minutes before unmolding.

Serves 4 to 6.

VARIATIONS: For a BROCCOLI CHEESE RING MOLD eliminate walnuts and substitute ⅓ to ½ cup grated cheese. Switzerland Swiss cheese gives an excellent flavor, but any firm grating cheese will do nicely. If using Parmesan cheese, reduce quantity to ¼ cup.

Chopped almonds can be used in place of walnuts.

Steamed Carrot Pudding

1½ cups scraped and
    coarsely chopped
    carrots (6 to 8 large
    carrots)
1 cup flour
2 teaspoons baking
    powder
½ teaspoon salt
¼ teaspoon baking soda
¼ teaspoon nutmeg
¼ teaspoon cinnamon

2 eggs separated
2 tablespoons lemon
    juice
½ cup butter at room
    temperature
2 tablespoons sour cream
    or heavy cream
½ cup brown sugar
Butter and fine, dry
    bread crumbs for mold

Generously butter a 1½-quart pudding mold, including the inside of lid. Add about 1 tablespoon bread crumbs. Replace lid and shake vigorously so that the entire surface is coated. Shake out excess bread crumbs. Set aside.

Preheat oven to 350°F.

Place about half of the carrots at a time in container of electric blender and blend until grated. (Or leave scraped carrots whole and grate through the coarse side of a hand grater.)

Place grated carrots in a large mixing bowl and add flour, baking powder, salt, baking soda, nutmeg and cinnamon. Mix thoroughly.

Place egg yolks, lemon juice, butter, cream and sugar into container of electric blender and blend until smooth. (Or cream butter with sugar, add egg yolks, cream and lemon juice. Beat with whisk until well blended.)

Add egg yolk mixture to carrot mixture and blend well.

Beat egg whites until stiff and fold into carrot mixture.

Pour into prepared mold. Place mold on a rack in a large pot and pour in sufficient water to cover bottom of pot by about 2 inches. Place pot over low heat, cover and let steam 45 to 50 minutes, or until firm.

Allow to stand about 3 minutes, then unmold onto a heated platter.

Serves 6 to 8.

Steamed Spinach Soufflé

2 cups cooked fresh or
    thawed frozen spinach,
    well drained and
    pressed dry
4 tablespoons flour
½ teaspoon baking
    powder
1 teaspoon salt

¼ teaspoon pepper
1 teaspoon lemon juice
½ cup beef stock or
    chicken stock from
    which all fat has been
    removed
4 eggs, separated

Generously butter the inside of a 2-quart metal pudding mold, including the inside of the lid. Chill.

Put the spinach, flour, baking powder, salt, pepper, lemon juice, stock and egg yolks into the container of an electric blender. Blend until thoroughly mixed.

Beat the egg whites until stiff and fold into the spinach mixture.

Pour into the prepared mold. Place mold on a rack in a large pot and pour in sufficient water to cover bottom of pot by about 2 inches. Place over moderate heat. Steam for 1½ hours, or until firm.

Unmold onto a heated serving plate, sprinkle with Parmesan cheese and serve at once.

Serves 6.

NOTE: If you do not have a blender, finely chop cooked fresh or frozen spinach, and beat ingredients together until well blended. Beat egg whites until stiff and proceed as directed.

Squash Ring Mold

1 12-ounce package
    frozen squash
3 tablespoons butter
3 tablespoons flour
1 cup milk

4 tablespoons sour cream
½ teaspoon salt
¼ teaspoon pepper
Pinch nutmeg (optional)
4 eggs, separated

Generously grease a 1½-quart ring mold with soft butter. Chill. Preheat oven to 375°F.

Cook squash according to package directions, but until very soft. Drain if necessary, then mash to a purée. Set aside.

Melt butter in a saucepan and stir in flour. When blended slowly add milk, stirring until smooth. Add sour cream and cook, stirring, to a thick sauce. Do not allow mixture to boil after adding sour cream. Season with salt and pepper and nutmeg if desired. Blend in puréed squash. Remove from heat and cool slightly, then add egg yolks, one at a time, beating well after each addition.

Beat egg whites until stiff. Fold in puréed squash.

Pour into prepared mold. Set mold in a baking dish and pour in sufficient hot water to come halfway up sides of mold.

Bake in preheated oven until firm—30 to 45 minutes.

Unmold and serve as a luncheon entree or as a vegetable to accompany roast beef, steak or baked chicken, or if desired fill center of ring with creamed seafood, chicken or ham.

Serves 6.

Tomato Ring Mold with Peas and Mushrooms

4 tablespoons butter	3 tablespoons grated
1 slice of Italian purple	Swiss cheese
onion, chopped	4 eggs, separated
6 medium tomatoes	1 cup chopped mush-
1 bay leaf	rooms (canned or
1 teaspoon salt	fresh)
½ teaspoon freshly	1 10-ounce package
ground black pepper	frozen peas
4 tablespoons flour	2 tablespoons heavy
	cream

Grease a 1½-quart ring mold with butter. Refrigerate until ready to use.

Preheat oven to 350°F.

Heat 1 tablespoon of butter in a medium saucepan and sauté the onion until very limp.

Peel the tomatoes by dipping into boiling water for a moment, then slipping off the skins with the tip of a small sharp knife.

Chop the tomatoes coarsely and add the sautéed onion. Add bay leaf, salt and pepper. Simmer over very low heat, stirring often, until tomatoes are reduced to a sauce—about 15 minutes. Set aside to cool.

Heat 2 tablespoons of the remaining butter in a shallow sauce-, pan or skillet over low heat. When bubbly, add flour, stirring quickly to avoid lumping.

Add the tomato mixture and cheese. Continue to cook, stirring, until smooth and slightly thick. Set aside to cool. Beat the egg yolks until frothy and add 1 cup of the tomato sauce. Blend well, then add to remaining tomato mixture, stirring well to blend.

Beat the egg whites until stiff but not dry, and gently fold tomato mixture into beaten whites.

Pour into mold and set into a pan of hot water.

Bake in preheated oven 25 to 35 minutes, or until firm.

Melt the last tablespoon of butter in a small saucepan and sauté mushrooms until tender. Add frozen peas and cook until heated through. Pour in cream and blend. Keep hot over very low heat until tomato ring is unmolded.

When ready to serve, unmold ring onto serving platter (loosen edges first with a table knife) and fill center with mushrooms and peas. Garnish with chopped chives, if desired.

Serves 6 to 8.

TIMBALES

Corn and Cheese Timbales (Budget)

1 16-ounce can cream-style corn	½ teaspoon coarsely ground black pepper
½ cup grated sharp cheddar cheese	1 teaspoon dry mustard
¼ teaspoon salt	3 large eggs, separated

Grease 6 timbale molds with butter.

Preheat oven to 325° F.

Combine corn, cheese, salt, pepper, mustard and egg yolks. Blend well.

Beat egg whites until stiff. Fold in corn mixture.

Pour into prepared molds. Place molds in a baking pan and pour in sufficient hot water to come halfway up sides of molds.

Bake in preheated oven until firm—about 30 minutes.

Unmold and serve with little link sausages.

Serves 6.

Timbales aux Petits Pois

1 10-ounce package frozen petits pois (deluxe tiny green peas)	1 tablespoon grated Parmesan cheese
3 tablespoons butter	½ teaspoon salt
3 tablespoons flour	¼ teaspoon pepper
1 cup milk	Pinch grated nutmeg
	4 eggs

Generously grease 6 timbale molds. Chill.

Preheat oven to 350°F.

Thaw peas.

Melt the butter in a saucepan and stir in the flour. When blended, slowly add milk, stirring constantly. Cook, stirring to a smooth and thick sauce. Stir in cheese and add seasonings. Remove from heat.

Place thawed peas in container of electric blender and blend for a few seconds until coarsely chopped, not puréed. Or place peas in a large wooden salad bowl and coarsely chop with a hand chopper or sharp knife. Add chopped peas to sauce.

Separate eggs. To sauce and peas add yolks, one at a time, stirring well after each addition.

Beat whites until stiff and fold in sauce and peas.

Pour into prepared molds. Place molds in a baking pan and pour in sufficient hot water to come halfway up sides of molds.

Bake until firm—about 30 minutes.

Unmold and serve as an accompaniment to any meat or fish with which peas are compatible. Can also be served with glazed carrots and tiny white onions as a main course luncheon entree. Serves 6.

Spinach Timbales

2 10-ounce packages frozen chopped spinach	1 tablespoon minced onion
3 tablespoons butter	3 eggs, well beaten
3 tablespoons flour	1 tablespoon lemon juice
1 cup milk	1 teaspoon salt

Lightly grease 6 individual timbale molds or a 1-quart ring mold.

Preheat oven to 375°F.

Place frozen spinach in a colander over a bowl and let thaw completely. Use a wooden spoon to press out all moisture. Thawing will take several hours. (If you are pressed for time, cook spinach according to package directions. Drain into a colander and press out all liquid.)

Melt butter in a saucepan and stir in flour. Slowly add milk, stirring as it is added. Cook, stirring, until mixture thickens. Remove from heat. Add remaining ingredients to well-drained spinach and blend thoroughly.

Pour mixture into individual timbale molds or ring mold. Place in a baking pan and pour in hot water to a depth of 1 inch.

Bake in preheated oven until firm—about 10 minutes for Timbale molds, 30 minutes for 1-quart mold.

Serves 6.

NOTE: The ring mold may be filled with creamed chicken, shrimp or lobster. The individual molds, topped with a cheese or tomato sauce, can be the stars of a vegetable luncheon or supper.

COLD SALADS

Molded salads is one area in which the imaginative cook, even if short on culinary techniques, can be fanciful and creative without fear of sauces curdling, soufflés collapsing, meats under- or overcooking, or cakes falling.

Once the basic principles of preparing molded salads are mastered, you will find them "sure fire and never fail."

The recipes in this section include basic gelatin salads, which are adaptable to taste preferences, to what you have on hand, and to your total menu as well. I've also included what I feel are the best of my molded salad collection, all of which are also adaptable. You can season to taste and substitute ingredients— just hold constant the basic liquid and solid proportions.

The variety of molded salads is literally endless, ranging from hearty main course dishes to light vegetable or fruit combinations. Moreover, molded salads can often make good use of leftovers—those little bits of this and that can be transformed into elegant looking and great tasting dishes. Extra easy to prepare, and taking less time to make than to describe, they are a wonderful answer for the busy or inexperienced cook.

ENTREE SALADS

Bloody Mary Ring Mold

2 envelopes unflavored
   gelatin
3 cups (non-alcoholic)
   Bloody Mary mix
3 tablespoons lemon
   juice
2–3 dashes Tabasco
   sauce
½ teaspoon Worcester-
   shire sauce

¼ teaspoon salt
¾ cup finely chopped
   celery
¼ cup finely chopped
   green pepper
PICKLED SHRIMP FILLING—
   see Sauces and
   Accompaniments

Chill a 1½-quart ring mold.

Sprinkle gelatin over ½ cup of the Bloody Mary mix in a large mixing bowl. Heat remaining Bloody Mary mix to boiling point. Pour over softened gelatin and stir until gelatin is dissolved. Stir in lemon juice, Tabasco, Worcestershire sauce and salt. Chill until thickened. Fold in celery and green pepper.

Rinse chilled mold with cold water. Pour in gelatin mixture. Chill until firm.

Unmold onto chilled platter and fill center with PICKLED SHRIMP FILLING, or as desired.

Serves 8 to 10.

Egg Salad Ring

12 large hard-cooked eggs	1 6-ounce package cream
½ small green pepper,	cheese at room tem-
seeded with all white	perature
removed	½ cup mayonnaise
2 stalks celery	¼ cup chili sauce
2–3 sprigs parsley	1 envelope unflavored
1 green onion	gelatin
½ cup mixed sweet	¼ cup cold water
pickles, well drained	½ teaspoon salt
1 7-ounce can pimento	½ teaspoon white pepper
strips, well drained	

Grease a 2-quart ring mold lightly with mayonnaise. Refrigerate until ready to use.

Grate the hard-cooked yolks or force through a fine sieve into a large mixing bowl.

Finely chop the egg whites, green pepper, celery, parsley, onion and pickles. Add to egg yolks. Coarsely chop and add pimento strips.

In a separate bowl, mash cream cheese until smooth, then fold in mayonnaise and chili sauce.

Sprinkle gelatin over cold water in top of a double boiler. Let stand for a few minutes to soften. Place over simmering water and stir until dissolved. Stir into cream cheese mixture.

Combine cream cheese with egg and vegetable mixture, and blend well. Stir in salt and pepper.

Spoon into prepared mold and refrigerate for about 4 hours, or until ready to serve.

Unmold and fill center with green salad.

Serves 8 to 12.

Tuna Salad Ring

1 1-pound can tunafish	Pepper
¾ cup finely diced celery	1 teaspoon Worcester-
1 tablespoon minced	shire sauce
onion	1 tablespoon horse-
¼ cup finely minced	radish
parsley	2–3 dashes Tabasco sauce
2 tablespoons lemon	2 envelopes unflavored
juice	gelatin
1 cup mayonnaise	¼ cup cold water
Salt	½ cup sour cream

Chill a 2-quart ring mold.

In a large bowl break up and flake tunafish. Add celery, onion, parsley, lemon juice and ¾ cup of the mayonnaise. Season with salt and pepper. Blend well. Chill.

To remaining mayonnaise add the Worcestershire sauce, horseradish and Tabasco.

Sprinkle gelatin over cold water in a small saucepan. Let stand a minute to soften, then stir over low heat until dissolved. Stir into mayonnaise sauce mixture. Add the sour cream and blend well.

Rinse chilled mold with cold water. Put in enough of the mayonnaise mixture to cover the bottom of the mold by about ½ inch and spread up the sides of the mold. Chill until firm.

Fill center with tuna mixture, mounding it around center of ring, not touching sides of mold. Spread remaining mayonnaise mixture over top. Chill until firm.

Serves 6 to 8.

NOTE: If mayonnaise gelatin stiffens too much to pour or spread at any time, place bowl in a pan of hot water and stir until sufficiently liquid.

Spanish Tuna Salad

1 6-ounce package
    lemon gelatin
1 tablespoon salt
2 cups boiling water
1 cup cold water
¼ cup dry sherry
3 tablespoons vinegar
⅛ teaspoon ground black
    pepper

½ cup tomato, diced,
    seeded and well
    drained
½ cup chopped pimento-
    stuffed olives
2 tablespoons minced
    scallion
1 7-ounce can tuna, well
    drained and broken
    into chunks

Chill six 1-cup individual molds.

Dissolve gelatin and salt in boiling water. Add cold water, sherry, vinegar and pepper. Chill until thickened. Blend in remaining ingredients.

Rinse chilled molds with cold water. Pour in gelatin mixture. Chill until firm—at least 4 hours, or overnight.

Unmold. Serve with mayonnaise.

Serves 6.

Turkey Salad

1 3-ounce package
    lemon gelatin
1 envelope unflavored
    gelatin
¼ teaspoon salt
1 cup boiling water
½ cup cold water
¼ cup mayonnaise
½ cup sour cream
1-2 tablespoons vinegar
    or lemon juice

1 tablespoon grated
    onion
Dash of pepper
1½ cups diced cooked
    turkey
⅓ cup chopped cucum-
    ber or green pepper
⅓ cup chopped celery
2 tablespoons chopped
    pimento

Chill a 1-quart decorative mold.

Dissolve gelatins and salt in boiling water. Add cold water, mayonnaise, sour cream, vinegar or lemon juice, onion and pepper. Beat until well blended. Pour into an 8-inch square pan. Freeze 15 to 20 minutes, or until firm to about 1 inch in from edge, but soft in center.

Spoon mixture into bowl and whip until fluffy. Fold in turkey and chopped vegetables.

Rinse chilled mold with cold water. Pour gelatin mixture into prepared mold. Chill until firm—30 to 60 minutes.

Unmold. Garnish with salad greens and serve with additional mayonnaise, if desired.

Makes 4 to 6 servings.

FRUIT AND VEGETABLE SALADS

Artichoke Salad

1 9-ounce package
frozen artichoke hearts
1 cup sliced fresh mush-
rooms (about ¼
pound)
1 cup prepared Italian
salad dressing
1 3-ounce package
lemon or lime
gelatin

1 cup boiling water
2 teaspoons vinegar
¾ cup dry white wine or
cold water
1 tablespoon sliced
pimento
½ cup mayonnaise

Chill a 1-quart round-bottomed mold.

Cook artichoke hearts as directed on package. Drain and combine with mushrooms in a bowl. Pour dressing over vegetables,
refrigerate and allow to marinate for at least 1 hour. Drain, reserving marinade.

Dissolve gelatin in boiling water. Add vinegar and wine or cold
water. Chill until thickened.

Drain mushrooms and artichoke hearts and reserve marinade.
Fold vegetables and pimento into gelatin mixture.

Rinse chilled mold with cold water. Pour in gelatin mixture.
Chill until firm—about 4 hours.

Unmold salad. Serve with mayonnaise mixed with reserved
marinade.

Makes 4 to 6 servings.

Carrot, Celery and Olive Salad

1 3-ounce package
lemon gelatin
1 envelope unflavored
gelatin
¼ teaspoon salt
1 cup boiling water
¾ cup canned carrot
juice

2 teaspoons vinegar
1 cup sour cream
1 cup shredded carrots
¼ cup diced celery
2 tablespoons sliced
black olives

Chill a 1½-quart decorative mold.

Dissolve gelatins and salt in boiling water. Stir in carrot juice and vinegar. Chill until thickened. Stir in sour cream, carrots, celery and olives.

Rinse chilled mold with cold water. Spoon in gelatin mixture. Chill until firm—about 4 hours.

Unmold. Garnish with crisp salad greens.

Serves 6 to 8.

Molded Coleslaw

1 3-ounce package
lemon gelatin
1 envelope unflavored
gelatin
½ teaspoon salt
1 cup boiling water
2 tablespoons cider
vinegar
½ cup mayonnaise

½ cup sour cream
1 tablespoon prepared
mustard
2 cups shredded
cabbage
½ cup minced tart apple
½ cup grated carrot
1 teaspoon grated onion

Chill a 1½-quart mold.

Combine gelatins with salt in a large mixing bowl. Add boiling water and stir until dissolved. Stir in vinegar, mayonnaise, sour cream and mustard. Chill until thickened. Fold in remaining ingredients.

Rinse chilled mold with cold water. Pour in coleslaw mixture. Chill until firm—about 4 hours.

Unmold and serve with sour cream combined equally with mayonnaise.

Serves 6 to 8.

Cranberry Apple Salad Mold

2 3-ounce packages red gelatin, any flavor
1 envelope unflavored gelatin
¼ teaspoon salt
1½ cups boiling water
½ cup Calvados, apple-jack or unsweetened apple juice
1 16-ounce can jellied cranberry sauce

2 tablespoons grated orange rind
2 medium tart apples, finely chopped (about 1 cup)
¾ cup chopped walnuts
WHIPPED CREAM MAYON-NAISE—see Sauces and Accompaniments

Chill a 1½-quart decorative mold.

Dissolve gelatins and salt in boiling water. Add Calvados, applejack or apple juice. Stir cranberry sauce with fork until smooth. Add to gelatin with orange rind, blending well. Chill until thickened. Add apples and nuts.

Rinse chilled mold with cold water. Pour in gelatin mixture. Chill until firm—about 4 hours.

Unmold. Garnish with WHIPPED CREAM MAYONNAISE.

Serves 6 to 8.

Cucumber Sour Cream Mold

2 medium cucumbers,
  peeled and coarsely
  grated (about 1½
  cups)
1 3-ounce package
  lemon or lime gelatin
1 teaspoon salt
1 cup boiling water
¾ cup cold water

2 teaspoons vinegar
½ cup sour cream
1 tablespoon minced
  green onion
1 tablespoon minced
  parsley
⅛ teaspoon coarsely
  ground black pepper

Chill a 1-quart decorative mold or 6 individual molds.

Wrap grated cucumbers in a clean cloth or absorbent paper and squeeze tightly to remove juice. Let drain completely.

Meanwhile, dissolve gelatin and salt in boiling water. Add cold water and vinegar. Blend in sour cream. Chill until thickened. Fold in drained cucumbers, onion, parsley and pepper.

Rinse chilled mold with cold water. Pour in mixture. Chill until firm—about 4 hours.

Serves 6.

Guacamole Mold

½ cup cold water
2 envelopes unflavored
  gelatin
½ cup boiling water
2 large, ripe avocados,
  peeled, seeded and cut
  into large pieces

3 tablespoons lemon
  juice
½ teaspoon grated onion
¾ cup sour cream
¼ cup chili sauce
3–4 drops Tabasco sauce
⅛ teaspoon salt

Rinse a 1-quart mold with cold water and place in refrigerator to chill.

Blender method:

Place cold water and gelatin in container of electric blender and blend at low speed until gelatin has softened. Pour in boiling water and blend a few seconds until gelatin has dissolved. If gelatin granules cling to sides of blender container, use a rubber spatula to push them to center and blend briefly. Add remaining ingredients and blend at high speed until smooth.

To prepare without blender:

Mash avocados until smooth.

Sprinkle gelatin over cold water to soften and add boiling water. Stir until gelatin has dissolved. Stir into mashed avocado. Add remaining ingredients and beat until well blended and smooth.

Pour mixture into a chilled mold and refrigerate until firm.

Serve as an appetizer accompanied by corn chips, as a first course or as a luncheon salad.

Serves 6 to 8.

Pear Salad

1 16-ounce can pear halves	¼ cup dry white wine
1 3-ounce package lime gelatin	1 tablespoon lemon juice
¼ teaspoon salt	2 3-ounce packages cream cheese
¾ cup boiling water	⅛ teaspoon ginger

Chill a 1-quart decorative mold.

Drain pears, reserving ¾ cup of the syrup. Coarsely dice pears and set aside.

Dissolve gelatin and salt in boiling water. Stir in pear syrup, wine and lemon juice.

Rinse chilled mold with cold water. Measure 1¼ cups of gelatin mixture into prepared mold. Chill until set but not firm— about 1 hour.

Meanwhile, whip cheese until creamy. Very slowly blend in remaining gelatin, beating until smooth. Carefully blend in ginger and pears. Spoon over set gelatin in mold. Chill until firm—about 4 hours.

Unmold and garnish with parsley or watercress. Serve with mayonnaise, if desired.

Serves 6.

Potato Salad Mold

6 *medium boiling pota-*
toes, sufficient to make
about 4 cups cubed
potatoes (The thin-
skinned, waxy ones
are best.)

2 *tablespoons cider*
vinegar

3 *tablespoons mild*
salad oil

Salt

Pepper

1 *cup finely chopped*
celery

1 *tablespoon minced*
chives or green onions

½ *cup finely diced mixed*
pickles

1 *envelope unflavored*
gelatin

¼ *cup lemon juice*

1 *cup mayonnaise*

1 *teaspoon prepared*
mustard

Rinse a 2-quart round-bottomed mold with cold water and place in refrigerator to chill.

Boil unpeeled potatoes in sufficient water to cover by about 2 inches until they can be easily pierced by a small sharp knife. Don't overcook or they will fall apart when sliced. Drain and peel while still hot. To protect your hands peel each potato quickly while holding under cold running water. Blot dry as soon as peeled and cut into bite-sized cubes (about 1 inch). Place in a large mixing bowl and add vinegar and oil. Season lightly with salt and pepper. Gently toss with two forks to blend. Set aside until cool. Add celery, chives or green onions, and diced mixed pickles. Cover and refrigerate until chilled.

Sprinkle gelatin over lemon juice in top of double boiler and let soften for 1 to 2 minutes. Place over simmering water and stir until gelatin is dissolved. Remove from heat and stir in mayonnaise and mustard. Blend into potato mixture.

When salad is well blended, spoon into a chilled mold. Cover and refrigerate for several hours until set.

Unmold onto lettuce-lined platter.

Serves 6 to 8.

Jellied Salad Niçoise

1 7-ounce can tunafish, drained and coarsely flaked	1 3-ounce package lemon gelatin
1 small tomato, diced and drained	1 teaspoon salt
½ cup cooked green beans	1 cup boiling water
2 tablespoons sliced ripe olives	1 cup cold water
2 tablespoons green pepper strips	2 teaspoons vinegar
2 tablespoons red onion strips	1 hard-cooked egg, diced
2 tablespoons mild French or Italian dressing	2 cups shredded lettuce
	ANCHOVY DRESSING—see Sauces and Accompaniments

Chill a 1½-quart decorative mold.

Combine tuna, vegetables, and salad dressing in a bowl. Mix lightly. Let stand.

Dissolve gelatin and salt in boiling water. Add cold water and vinegar. Chill until mixture just begins to thicken.

Rinse mold in cold water. Spoon vegetable mixture and diced egg into prepared mold. Pour on half the gelatin. Spread lettuce on top. Add remaining gelatin. Chill until firm—at least 4 hours.

Unmold salad. Garnish with watercress, if desired. Serve with ANCHOVY DRESSING.

Makes 4 to 6 servings.

Molded Vegetable and Apple Salad

1 3-ounce package lemon gelatin	2–3 dashes Tabasco sauce
2 chicken bouillon cubes	1 cup sour cream
½ teaspoon salt	½ cup diced tart apples
1 cup boiling water	½ cup diced celery
2 tablespoons tarragon vinegar	¼ cup diced radishes
	¼ cup diced cucumbers

Chill a 1-quart decorative mold or 4 to 6 individual molds.

Place gelatin, bouillon cubes and salt in a mixing bowl. Add boiling water and stir until dissolved. Stir in vinegar and Tabasco. Chill until slightly thickened. Blend in sour cream and remaining ingredients.

Pour into mold or molds. Chill until firm—about 4 hours.

Unmold and garnish with lettuce or watercress. Serve with mayonnaise or French dressing.

Serves 4 to 6.

ASPIC SALADS

Basic (Or Not So Basic) Aspic

2 envelopes unflavored
gelatin
⅓ cup cold water
¾ cup boiling chicken,
beef or fish stock, or
clam or tomato juice
1½ cups room tempera-
ture chicken, beef or
fish stock, or clam or
tomato juice
2 tablespoons vinegar,
strained lemon juice,
dry white wine, cognac
or brandy
2–3 tablespoons mayon-
naise, sour cream or
heavy cream
Salt, celery salt, seasoned
salt, Tabasco sauce,
Worcestershire sauce
or horseradish (op-
tional, to taste)

A combination, totaling 2
cups, of any of the fol-
lowing: chopped cu-
cumbers; chopped
celery; chopped
radishes; chopped tart
apples; diced cooked
chicken, turkey,
shrimp, lobster, or
flaked fish fillets; diced
cooked mixed
vegetables
MAYONNAISE COLÉE—see
Sauces and
Accompaniments

Chill a 1½- to 2-quart decorative mold.

Sprinkle gelatin over cold water. Let stand several minutes to soften. Add boiling liquid and stir until gelatin has dissolved. Add remaining liquid and chill until mixture thickens. Fold in, if desired, mayonnaise, sour cream or heavy cream. Season to taste.

Add a combination, totaling 2 cups, of any of the meats or vegetables listed.

Rinse chilled mold with cold water. Pour in gelatin mixture. Chill until firm.

Unmold and garnish. "Ice" aspic with MAYONNAISE COLÉE, if desired, or serve with basic or seasoned mayonnaise.

Serves 6 to 8.

Italian Salad in Aspic

2 envelopes unflavored
  gelatin
1 10-ounce can jellied
  chicken consomme
⅓ cup dry white wine
1 small cucumber,
  peeled and thinly
  sliced

1 16-ounce can Italian-
  style mixed vegetable
  salad
½ cup chopped celery

Rinse a 1-quart mold with cold water and place in refrigerator to chill.

Sprinkle gelatin over ½ cup of the consomme to soften. Place remaining consomme with wine in a saucepan and bring to a full boil. Add softened gelatin. Remove from heat and stir until gelatin has dissolved. Cool, then refrigerate until aspic mixture begins to thicken. Stir often for even consistency.

Rinse mold with cold water. Pour in a thin layer of gelatin to line mold. Refrigerate until set but not quite firm. Arrange cucumber slices attractively on surface. Cover with a second thin layer of gelatin. Refrigerate until set.

Drain liquid from vegetable salad. Blot dry with paper toweling. Combine with celery and fold into remaining thickened gelatin.

Pour into aspic-lined mold. Refrigerate several hours, or until ready to serve.

Unmold onto lettuce-lined platter and serve with Italian mayonnaise.

Serves 6 to 8.

Classic Tomato Aspic Ring

A tomato aspic ring mold is always an effective way to present the salad part of a buffet, but so often it's a taste disappointment —very bland and lacking in flavor. Guests eat the center and push the aspic aside. Not with this recipe. It's not a "shortcut," but neither is it difficult or really time consuming to prepare; and, as people really enjoy it, I find it well worth the small effort.

3 cups tomato juice	1 teaspoon seasoned salt
1 cup clear, fat-free chicken stock	1 teaspoon salt
	1 teaspoon sugar
1 thick slice mild purple onion	2 envelopes unflavored gelatin
Several leafy celery tops	¼ cup lemon juice, strained
2–3 sprigs parsley	
2 whole cloves	3–4 dashes Tabasco sauce
2 bay leaves	

Chill a 2-quart ring mold.

In a saucepan combine tomato juice, chicken stock, onion, celery tops, parsley, cloves, bay leaves, seasoned salt, salt and sugar. Simmer, uncovered, over low heat for about 15 minutes.

Sprinkle gelatin over lemon juice in a large mixing bowl. Let stand several minutes to soften.

Strain hot tomato-stock mixture into softened gelatin. Stir until gelatin is dissolved. Blend in Tabasco sauce.

Rinse chilled mold with cold water. Pour in aspic mixture. Chill until firm—2 to 3 hours.

Unmold and fill center as desired.

Serves 6 to 8.

NOTE: Recipe may be doubled, but decrease gelatin to 3 envelopes instead of 4.

You can fill the center of a tomato aspic ring with any well-seasoned, well-made salad: with shrimp, seafood, or chicken; with cooked marinated vegetables, green salad or coleslaw; or with cottage cheese nicely seasoned with Worcestershire and Tabasco sauce, and mixed with finely chopped radishes, celery, green pepper and tart apple.

STEAMED BREADS
AND PUDDINGS

These are among the easiest and most satisfactory of all desserts to prepare. They are less rich than pies or cakes, yet they still make a satisfying ending to what might otherwise be a light meal. Once you try a few of the recipes included here, you will probably want to experiment with variations of your own. Almost any fruit or flavoring may be used. Two additional points in favor of puddings should be noted. They are both economical and non-temperamental about waiting to be served either hot or cold.

Classic Boston Brown Bread

½ cup chopped walnuts
½ cup seedless raisins
1 cup stone-ground
  whole wheat flour
1 cup yellow cornmeal
1 cup rye flour
½ teaspoon salt

½ teaspoon cinnamon
2 teaspoons baking soda
2 cups buttermilk or 2
  cups milk mixed with
  2 teaspoons vinegar
¾ cup dark molasses

Generously grease two 1-quart cylindrical molds, including inside of lids, with soft butter.

Bring all ingredients to room temperature.

Mix walnuts and raisins with whole wheat flour. Add cornmeal, rye flour, salt, cinnamon and baking soda. Mix thoroughly.

Combine buttermilk (or soured milk) and molasses. Stir into dry ingredients and blend well.

Pour batter into prepared molds. Cover and place in a large heavy pot on a rack or crumpled round of foil. Add sufficient water to cover bottom of pot. Cover pot and place over medium heat until water boils, then lower heat until water simmers gently. Steam the bread for 3 hours, adding additional hot water as needed to maintain original level.

Unmold and cool before slicing.

NOTE: You may substitute 1 cup raisins for the ½ cup each of walnuts and raisins, or a second cup of whole wheat flour for the rye flour. The results will be an excellent steamed bread, lighter in both flavor and texture than the classic recipe.

Steamed Date Nut Bread

1 cup chopped dates
1 cup chopped walnuts
1⅓ cups whole wheat flour
(or substitute ¾ cup
all-purpose flour and
¼ cup toasted wheat
germ)
⅓ teaspoon each ginger,
nutmeg and allspice

1 tablespoon baking
powder
½ teaspoon salt
5 tablespoons butter
1 cup light brown sugar
1 egg
1 cup milk

Generously grease a 1½-quart cylindrical mold, including the inside of lid, with soft butter.

Combine dates, walnuts and ⅓ cup flour. Blend well. Mix in remaining flour, spices, baking powder and salt.

In a separate bowl cream the butter with the brown sugar. Add the egg and beat well. Add flour mixture alternately with milk, about ⅓ at a time, blending well after each addition.

Pour into prepared mold. Cover and place in a large heavy pot on a rack or a crumpled round of foil. Pour in sufficient hot water to cover bottom of pot. Cover pot, place over medium heat and bring water to a full boil, then lower heat so that water simmers gently. Steam bread for 2 hours. Add additional hot water if necessary.

Unmold and cool before slicing.

Makes about 12 slices.

Blackberry Pudding

1 1-pound can black-
   berries in syrup
2½ cups firmly packed
   bread crumbs (¼-inch
   thick) (6 to 8 slices day
   old bread, crust
   removed)

3 eggs
½ cup sugar
½ cup light cream
1 tablespoon kirsch (or
   substitute any orange
   liqueur or brandy)

Generously butter a 2-quart pudding mold, including inside of lid. Add about 2 tablespoons sugar, cover and shake vigorously so that the entire surface is coated with sugar. Shake out any excess sugar. Set aside.

Drain blackberries, reserving ½ cup syrup.

Place a layer of bread crumbs in the bottom of the prepared mold and cover with a layer of blackberries. Continue layering until all the bread crumbs and blackberries have been used. End with a layer of bread.

Beat eggs until blended. Add sugar and beat with a wire whisk or electric hand beater until sugar is dissolved. Add cream, blackberry syrup and kirsch. Blend and pour mixture slowly over the layers of bread and blackberries. Cover the mold and place on a rack or crumpled round of foil in a heavy pot. Add sufficient hot water to cover bottom of pot by 2 inches. Steam for 1½ hours; add additional water if necessary.

Remove mold from water and let stand 2 or 3 minutes. Unmold onto serving platter.

Serve hot or at room temperature with sweetened whipped cream, vanilla ice cream or sabayon sauce.

Serves 6.

Fourth of July Cherry Firecrackers

This is a wonderful surprise ending for a Fourth of July buffet supper—an easy but spectacular red, white and blue dessert.

3 cups firmly packed
white bread cubes (12
to 18 slices firm white
bread, crusts re-
moved)

2½ cups pitted Bing
cherries, fresh or
canned and drained

3 eggs
1 cup sugar
1¼ cups milk
2 tablespoons Grand
Marnier

BLUEBERRY SAUCE—see
Sauces and
Accompaniments

Generously butter the insides and lids of two 1-quart cylindrical molds. Dust with granulated sugar.

Place a layer of bread cubes in the bottom of each mold, cover with a layer of cherries, repeat the layers until molds are ⅔ full and end with a layer of bread cubes.

Using a wire whisk, lightly beat the eggs and sugar. Slowly stir in the milk and liqueur, and whip gently until well blended.

Pour the egg-milk mixture evenly over the cherries and bread in the molds. Cover and set the molds on a rack or crumpled round of foil in a very large pot that will allow the steam to circulate freely. Pour in enough boiling water to cover the bottom of the pot. Bring to a full boil, then lower heat to a gentle simmer. Cover pot loosely to allow steam to escape and steam for 1½ hours. Add additional hot water if needed.

Unmold while still hot onto a serving platter. When puddings have cooled slightly, insert a tiny red birthday candle in each end for the "wick." When ready to serve, spoon BLUEBERRY SAUCE over surface and garnish with whipped cream, if desired. Light the wick of each candle for a flaming finale to the Glorious Fourth!

Serves 8 to 10.

Barbados Chocolate Pudding

An elegant soufflé-like pudding that can easily be made ahead and held for serving right in the steamer pot with no loss of its light but rich texture and taste.

8 squares semi-sweet
  chocolate
¼ cup rum
2 tablespoons orange
  marmalade
1 teaspoon grated lemon
  rind

1 tablespoon slivered
  almonds
½ cup sugar
8 egg whites
1 tablespoon fine bread
  crumbs
¼ teaspoon salt

Generously butter a 1-quart pudding mold and the inside of its lid. Add about 2 tablespoons of sugar, replace lid and shake vigorously to distribute sugar evenly.

Melt the chocolate with the rum in top half of a double boiler over gently simmering water. When melted, remove from heat and allow to cool to room temperature.

Combine marmalade, lemon rind, almonds, sugar and 2 of the egg whites in a large bowl. Beat with a wire whisk until well blended. Add the bread crumbs and melted chocolate. Blend well.

Using a wire whisk, beat the remaining egg whites with the salt until stiff but not dry.

Add 4 tablespoons of the whipped egg whites to the chocolate mixture and beat until blended. Gently fold in remaining egg whites.

Pour into prepared mold. Cover and place on rack in large, heavy pot. Pour in hot water to cover bottom of the pot by about 2 inches and bring to a boil. Lower heat to simmer and steam for about 1½ hours. Add additional hot water if necessary.

Mold may be left to stand in hot water (with heat turned off) up to 2 hours before serving or may be unmolded at once and refrigerated until ready to serve.

Garnish with whipped cream lightly flavored with rum.
Serves 4 to 6.

Steamed Chocolate Pudding

This pudding has the texture and taste of a chocolate soufflé. Unlike a soufflé, however, it can be prepared ahead and served hot, cold or at room temperature. I've prepared it many times and can safely say it never fails and always pleases.

2 *tablespoons butter*　　¼ *cup strong cold coffee,*
3 *tablespoons cocoa*　　　　*light rum, brandy or*
1 *tablespoon flour*　　　　　*any liqueur*
¾ *cup light cream*　　　3 *eggs*
¾ *cup sugar*

Generously butter a 1-quart metal pudding mold, including the inside of the rim. Add about 1 tablespoon sugar, place the lid on tightly and shake vigorously. Remove the lid and invert to remove any excess sugar.

Put the butter in a saucepan over low heat. When melted stir in the cocoa and flour. Blend in the cream and cook over low heat. Stir with a wooden spoon until mixture is smooth. Remove from heat and add sugar and coffee or liqueur. Beat until well blended. Cool slightly.

Separate the eggs. Add yolks to chocolate mixture one at a time, beating well after each addition.

Whip egg whites until stiff. (A wire whisk is best for this job.) Beat about 4 tablespoons of the beaten whites into the chocolate mixture. Gently fold chocolate mixture into remaining whites, blending thoroughly.

Carefully pour the pudding into the prepared mold and cover. Place on a rack or crumpled round of foil in a heavy pot. Pour in enough hot water to cover bottom of pot by 2 inches. Cover and steam for 1½ hours. Add additional hot water if necessary.

Remove mold from water and let stand about 2 minutes. Unmold and serve either hot, cold or at room temperature.

Serve with sweetened whipped cream or slightly softened vanilla ice cream.

Serves 6 to 8.

Old-Fashioned Christmas Pudding

1 large tart apple, diced
  (about ½ cup)
1 cup diced mixed
  candied fruit
½ cup raisins
1 teaspoon grated lemon
  rind
⅔ cup brandy or light
  rum
½ cup butter at room
  temperature
¾ cup sugar

3 eggs
¾ cup flour
½ cup fine graham
  cracker crumbs
½ teaspoon allspice
¼ teaspoon cinnamon
¼ cup finely minced beef
  suet
HARD SAUCE SHELLS—see
  Sauces and
  Accompaniments

Generously butter a .1-quart pudding mold, including cover. Add about 1 tablespoon flour, cover and shake the mold vigorously. Remove the lid, invert and shake out excess flour.

Peel, seed and finely dice the apple. Finely mince the candied fruit.

Combine raisins, chopped apple, minced candied fruit and grated lemon rind. Add the brandy or rum, and let soak several hours.

Cream the butter with the sugar until light and fluffy. Add the eggs one at a time, beating well after each addition. Add the flour and graham cracker crumbs. Add allspice, cinnamon, suet and liquor-soaked fruit. Blend well.

Pour into prepared mold. Place mold in large heavy pot on rack or crumpled round of foil. Pour in enough hot water to cover bottom of pot by 2 inches. Steam for 2½ to 3 hours; add more water if needed.

At this point the pudding may be unmolded and served immediately or refrigerated for several days while still in the mold, then resteamed until heated through.

To serve, unmold hot pudding onto a warm, flameproof platter. Sprinkle pudding with sugar. Heat ¼ cup brandy in a small saucepan over low heat. Ignite brandy and pour, flaming, over pudding. Take flaming pudding to table and serve at once with HARD SAUCE SHELLS, a rich vanilla custard, or vanilla ice cream. Serves 6 to 8.

Steamed Cranberry Pudding

4 *tablespoons butter*	2 *cups bread cubes made*
1 *cup milk*	*from day-old French*
3 *cups cranberries*	*bread, crusts removed*
1½ *cups sugar*	3 *eggs*
2 *tablespoons flour*	2 *teaspoons baking*
	powder

Grease a 2-quart pudding mold and lid generously with butter. Add about 1 tablespoon sugar, cover mold and shake vigorously. Uncover and shake out excess sugar.

Put butter and milk in a saucepan and stir over low heat until butter has melted. Set aside and cool until lukewarm.

Coarsely chop cranberries and combine in large bowl with the sugar, flour and bread cubes.

Add the eggs to the cooled milk and butter, and beat with a whisk until blended. Add this mixture to cranberry mixture and blend well. Stir in baking powder.

Pour batter into prepared mold. Cover and place mold in a large heavy pot on a rack or a crumpled round of foil. Add sufficient hot water to cover bottom of pot by 2 inches. Bring water to a boil, then adjust heat so that water simmers gently. Cover pan and let pudding steam for 1½ to 2 hours, or until firm. Add additional hot water if necessary.

Let stand about 5 minutes before unmolding.

Serves 6.

Creole Pineapple Pudding

1 8½-ounce can crushed
  pineapple
1 cup milk
2 tablespoons butter
⅓ cup flour

4 eggs, separated
2 tablespoons light rum
  or brandy (optional)

Grease the insides and lid of a 1½-quart pudding mold with soft butter. Add about 1 tablespoon sugar. Cover and shake mold vigorously. Remove lid and shake out excess sugar. Chill while preparing pudding.

Drain pineapple, reserving juice.

Heat the milk and butter until mixture comes to a boil. Remove from heat and stir in flour. Add egg yolks one at a time, beating well after each addition. Add ⅓ cup of the reserved pineapple juice and rum or brandy, if desired. Stir to a smooth batter.

Beat egg whites until stiff. Fold into batter.

Pour about ¼ of batter into prepared mold. Sprinkle with pineapple. Repeat layers until all batter and pineapple are used, ending with batter.

Place mold in a large pot on a rack or a crumpled round of foil. Add sufficient hot water to cover bottom of the pot by 2 inches. Bring water to a boil, then adjust heat so that water simmers gently. Cover pot. Let pudding steam for 1½ hours, or until firm. Add additional hot water if necessary. Unmold onto serving plate. Serve hot or cold.

Serves 6 to 8.

Bourbon Whiskey Pudding with Raisins

3½ cups white bread
  cubes (¼-inch thick),
  crusts removed
¾ cup seedless raisins
5 eggs
¾ cup light brown sugar·

1½ cups milk
½ cup bourbon whiskey
BOURBON SAUCE—see
Sauces and
Accompaniments

Grease the insides and lid of a 2-quart pudding mold with soft butter. Add about 1 tablespoon sugar, cover and shake vigorously. Remove lid and shake out excess sugar.

Put a layer of bread cubes into the bottom of the mold and sprinkle with raisins. Repeat until bread cubes and raisins are used.

In a mixing bowl beat eggs with brown sugar until sugar is well blended.

Heat the milk with the whiskey almost to the boiling point. Slowly add to the egg-sugar mixture, beating constantly as it is added.

Pour mixture slowly over bread crumbs and raisins. Cover mold and place on a rack or crumpled round of foil in a large pot. Add sufficient hot water to cover bottom of pot by 2 inches. Cover. Place over high heat and bring water to a full boil, then lower heat and simmer gently. Steam pudding for 1 hour. Add additional hot water if necessary.

Remove mold from water, uncover and let stand for about 5 minutes.

Unmold onto a serving platter. Serve hot, warm or cold with sweetened whipped cream, spiked with a little bourbon, or with BOURBON SAUCE.

Serves 6.

SPECIAL DESSERTS

The strong points of special molded desserts are not only their delicious taste and ease of preparation, but their festive and elegant appearance. Few guests will fail to be impressed by a PEACH MELBA RING, yet it's one—two—three—easy to make. For the super sophisticated or the guests who have had everything, try COEUR À LA CRÈME WITH FRAISES AU KIRSCH, one of the most delicate and delicious desserts ever created by the talented chefs of France.

CAKES

Rosace Cake

3 *whole eggs*	4 *tablespoons butter,*
½ *cup sugar*	*melted and cooled*
½ *teaspoon rose water*	2 *tablespoons ground*
1 *cup flour*	*almonds*
	2 *egg whites*

Generously butter a 1½-quart Rosace mold with soft butter. Sprinkle with flour.

Preheat oven to 350°F.

Place eggs, sugar and rose water in top of double boiler over simmering water and beat with a whisk until thick and about double in volume. Remove from heat and fold in flour, butter and ground almonds to make a stiff batter.

In a large bowl beat egg whites until stiff. Fold into batter mixture.

Pour into prepared molds. (Bake any excess batter in a plain pan or in muffin tins.) Bake 30 to 40 minutes, or until surface is lightly browned.

Let stand at room temperature about 5 minutes, then unmold onto cake rack to cool. Sprinkle with confectioners' sugar or cover with a pink-tinted frosting.

Makes one cake.

Savarin au Rum

SAVARIN

2 envelopes active dry yeast	2 tablespoons butter at room temperature
1 teaspoon sugar	2 tablespoons sugar
⅓ cup lukewarm water	3 large eggs
2 cups flour	1 cup milk

RUM SYRUP

¾ cup water	2 cloves
1 cup sugar	½ stick cinnamon
Strip of orange peel	½ cup light, dry rum
Strip of lemon peel	

Generously butter and flour a Savarin mold; shake out excess flour.

Blend yeast with sugar in a large mixing bowl. Add lukewarm water. Cover with a kitchen towel and let stand in a warm place for about 15 minutes.

Add 1¾ cups of the flour and remaining savarin ingredients. Mix well. Cover and let rise in a warm place until double in bulk, about 1 hour, then punch down and mix in remaining flour. Cover and again let rise until double in bulk, about 45 minutes. Punch dough down and turn into prepared mold. Let stand for about 1 hour to rise once again.

Preheat oven to 350°F.

When savarin has risen, place on middle rack of preheated oven and bake for 40 to 50 minutes, or until well browned and firm.

Unmold onto a cake rack to cool.

While cake cools, prepare syrup. Combine all ingredients except rum in a saucepan and stir constantly over medium heat until sugar dissolves. Simmer for about 20 minutes. Remove and discard orange and lemon peels, cloves and cinnamon. Stir in rum and cool to lukewarm.

Place cool savarin in a shallow pan and pour lukewarm rum syrup over surface. Let stand about 1 hour, turning cake several times to soak up the syrup.

Place savarin on serving plate and fill center with whipped cream and fresh strawberries, or dust savarin with powdered sugar and serve "as is." It's delicious simply sliced and served with good strong coffee.

Makes one cake.

Two-piece Cake Molds

Grease the mold very generously with soft sweet butter, mild oil or a combination of both. A pastry brush does the job best. Dust the greased surface with flour, invert and shake out excess flour. Fill the solid sections of the mold with the dough (recipes follow) to just below the joints. Move a wooden spoon gently through the dough to release any air bubbles, being careful not to disturb the greased and floured surface of the mold. (Insert wooden picks upright into the ears of rabbit molds where they join the head. Remember to remove when serving cake.) Put the lid on the mold, making sure it locks, and tie or wire lid and mold together so that steam from the rising dough does not force the two sections apart.

Preheat oven to 375°F. Put the filled mold on a cookie sheet and bake for about 1 hour. Test for doneness by inserting a thin metal skewer or food pick through a steam vent. Remove from oven and let mold stand on a rack for about 15 minutes. Carefully remove top of mold and continue to cool for about 5 minutes before unmolding.

Unmold onto cake rack and let stand until completely cooled. Place on a cookie sheet in freezer until very firm before icing. Use a firm but spreadable icing—see Sauces and Accompaniments. To define features, use nuts, cherries, raisins or candy drops.

I. For Bunnies and Lamb Molds

2 cups sifted cake flour
¼ teaspoon salt
2½ teaspoons baking
  powder
½ cup butter at room
  temperature

1 cup sugar
1 cup milk
1 teaspoon vanilla
  extract
2 large egg whites

Prepare a 1½-quart decorative mold as directed.
   Preheat oven to 375°F.
   Sift together flour, salt and baking powder.
   Cream butter with sugar. Beat until light and smooth.
   Add flour mixture alternately with milk to creamed butter. Stir in vanilla.
   Beat egg whites until stiff and fold them into batter.
   Fill and bake mold as directed. (Bake any leftover batter in muffin tins.)
   Unmold and ice as directed.

II. For Santa Claus Molds

2 cups sifted cake flour
¼ teaspoon salt
2½ teaspoons baking
  powder
½ cup butter
1 cup sugar

2 large eggs, well beaten
½ cup milk
½ teaspoon vanilla
  extract
¼ teaspoon almond
  extract

Prepare a 1½-quart mold as directed.
   Preheat oven to 375°F.
   Sift together flour, salt, and baking powder.
   Cream butter. Add sugar and beat until light and fluffy. (If the mixture is beaten until sugar dissolves, the cake will have a really superb texture.) Add the beaten eggs and mix well.
   Add flour mixture alternately with milk to butter-egg mixture, blending lightly after each addition. Stir in vanilla and almond extracts.

Pour into prepared mold. (Bake any leftover batter in muffin tins.) Bake for about 45 minutes.

Unmold and ice as directed.

Each recipe makes one cake.

MOUSSES

Maria's Carrot Mousse à la Orange

2 envelopes unflavored
    gelatin
½ cup strained orange
    juice
½ cup unsweetened
    pineapple juice
½ cup plus 2 tablespoons
    any good orange
    liqueur, such as
    Cointreau, Curaçao or
    Grand Marnier; if no
    liqueur is desired, use
    2 additional table-
    spoons orange juice

1 teaspoon chopped
    lemon rind
1 cup carrots, scraped
    and sliced
6 slices canned pine-
    apple, unsweetened

Refrigerate 6 individual molds or a 1-quart mold until chilled.

Sprinkle gelatin over ½ cup orange juice in container of electric blender. Allow to stand while assembling other ingredients.

In a small saucepan bring pineapple juice to a boil. While still hot pour over softened gelatin in blender and blend at low speed until gelatin has dissolved. If any gelatin granules stick to container, use a rubber spatula or wooden spoon to scrape them into mixture.

When gelatin is dissolved, add remaining ingredients and blend at high speed until carrots and pineapple are finely grated and mixture is almost, but not quite, smooth.

Rinse chilled molds with cold water and pour in carrot mixture. Refrigerate until firm (about 1 hour).

Unmold and serve with sweetened whipped cream.

Serves 6.

Coconut Mousse

2 envelopes unflavored
   gelatin
⅓ cup water
1 cup milk
½ cup sugar

1 cup grated coconut,
   canned or frozen
1 pint heavy cream
1 tablespoon dry sherry

Chill a 1½-quart decorative mold.

Sprinkle gelatin over water. Set aside to soften.

Heat milk just to boiling point. Add softened gelatin and sugar, and stir until dissolved. Remove from heat. Add coconut. Let mixture stand at room temperature until cool.

Beat cream until stiff. Fold in coconut mixture and sherry.

Rinse chilled mold with cold water. Pour in mousse mixture. Chill until firm (about 1 hour).

Unmold and serve.

Serves 6.

Classic Orange Mousse

4 egg yolks
1 cup sugar
½ cup strained orange
   juice
¼ cup Grand Marnier or
   any orange liqueur, or
   ¼ cup additional
   orange juice

1 teaspoon grated
   orange or lemon rind
½ pint heavy cream

Chill 8 individual molds or one 2-quart mold.

Place egg yolks and sugar in top of double boiler over simmering water and beat with an electric hand mixer, a rotary beater or wire whisk until very thick and about triple in volume. Remove from heat and beat in orange juice, liqueur and grated rind. Cool this custard to room temperature.

In a large mixing bowl beat cream with a wire whisk until stiff. Fold in custard mixture.

Rinse out chilled molds or mold with cold water. Pour in mousse mixture. Cover and seal tops with foil, then wrap and seal each mold completely in foil. Place in freezer until firm— about 3 hours.

Unmold onto a chilled platter about 1 hour before serving. Refrigerate until time to serve.

Serves 8.

Sherry Cream Mousse

PART I

3 *envelopes unflavored gelatin*	½ *cup sugar*
½ *cup cold water*	1½ *cups strained orange juice*
¾ *cup boiling water*	1½ *cups sherry*

Chill a shallow 2-quart oblong baking pan.

Sprinkle gelatin over cold water in a large bowl. Pour in boiling water and stir until gelatin is dissolved. Add sugar, orange juice and sherry. Stir until sugar has dissolved.

Rinse chilled pan. Pour in gelatin mixture. Chill until firm, about 1 hour. With a knife dipped in hot water, cut gelatin into small (about ½-inch) cubes.

PART II

1 *pint heavy cream*	1 *envelope unflavored gelatin*
2 *tablespoons confectioners' sugar*	⅓ *cup cold water*

Chill a 2-quart decorative mold.

Beat cream until stiff. Fold in confectioners' sugar.

In top of double boiler sprinkle gelatin over cold water and stir over simmering water until dissolved. Stir into whipped cream. Fold in about ¾ of the firm, diced, sherry gelatin.

Rinse chilled mold with cold water and pour in whipped cream-gelatin mixture. Chill until firm, about one hour.

Unmold and surround with remaining diced sherry jelly.

Serves 6 to 8.

Sour-Cream Pineapple Mousse

2 cups milk	2 envelopes unflavored
4 eggs	gelatin
½ cup sugar	¼ cup cold water
⅛ teaspoon salt	1 8-ounce can crushed
1 tablespoon kirsch,	pineapple, drained
Cointreau or light rum	½ cup sour cream

Chill a 1½-quart decorative mold.

Scald milk.

In top half of double boiler beat eggs with sugar until blended. Slowly add the scalded milk, beating constantly as it is added. Cook over simmering water, stirring often, to a smooth custard that is thick enough to coat the spoon. Blend in salt and liqueur.

Sprinkle gelatin over cold water. Let stand several minutes to soften, then add it to the hot custard and stir until dissolved. Cool to room temperature. Stir in pineapple and sour cream.

Rinse chilled mold with cold water. Pour in mousse mixture. Chill until firm.

Unmold and garnish with pineapple slices.

Serves 8.

RING MOLDS

Caramel Crisp Ring

6 tablespoons butter   6 cups cornflakes
1 cup brown sugar

Grease a 1½-quart ring mold generously with soft butter. Chill.
    Melt the butter in a large skillet. Add the sugar and cook over
very low heat, stirring to a smooth syrup. Add the cornflakes. Stir
and turn the flakes until all are completely coated with the sugar
mixture.
    Remove from heat. Spoon while still warm into the prepared
mold and press down firmly with the back of a wooden spoon.
Cool slightly, but do not allow to become cold. Unmold onto a
round platter. Do not refrigerate.
    When ready to serve fill center as desired—with sliced fresh
strawberries or peaches, any cooked fruit, or with whipped cream
or ice cream.
    Serves 6.

Caramel Custard Ring with Fruit

¾ cup sugar   4 whole eggs
3 cups milk at room   4 egg yolks
    temperature

Generously grease a 1½-quart ring mold with soft butter. Chill.
    Preheat oven to 375°F.
    Place ⅓ cup of sugar in a heavy saucepan and stir over low
heat until sugar dissolves to a pale golden syrup. Add the milk.

The sugar will harden to brittle. Stir until the brittle sugar dissolves. Remove from heat.

In a large mixing bowl beat the whole eggs, egg yolks and remaining sugar until well blended. Slowly add the caramel milk and blend well.

Pour into prepared mold. Place in a baking pan and pour sufficient hot water around mold to come halfway up sides of mold.

Place in preheated oven and bake for about 45 minutes until custard has set (a small pointed knife inserted in center will come out clean).

Let the custard stand at room temperature for about 15 minutes before unmolding.

Unmold onto a serving plate. Serve at room temperature or chill. Fill center with any fresh or canned fruit or fruit mixture that has been sweetened lightly with confectioners' sugar and marinated in a compatible liqueur.

Serves 6 to 8.

Chocolate Grand Marnier

½ pound semi-sweet chocolate	1½ cups grated almonds (about 5 ounces)
4 tablespoons Grand Marnier	1 tablespoon grated orange rind
½ pound unsalted butter at room temperature	10 to 12 Social Tea biscuits, crumbled
2 eggs, separated	Confectioners' sugar

Generously butter a 2-quart ring mold and refrigerate until ready to use.

Break the chocolate into small pieces. Place in top of double boiler over simmering water until soft. Add Grand Marnier and stir until chocolate is completely melted and mixture is smooth. Cool to room temperature.

Cream the butter until very light and fluffy. Add the egg yolks. Beat until thoroughly blended and as light as whipped cream.

Fold in the almonds and grated orange rind. Then blend in the cooled chocolate mixture.

In a separate bowl beat egg whites until stiff. Fold into chocolate mixture. Gently fold in crumbled tea biscuits.

Pour the mixture into the prepared mold. Rap the mold sharply once or twice on the table to settle mixture evenly and prevent air bubbles. Cover mold tightly with foil or plastic wrap and refrigerate 6 to 8 hours.

Unmold and dust surface with confectioners' sugar. Slice just before serving.

Serves 6.

Jamaican Flan Ring

1 medium-sized ripe	5 eggs
pineapple	3½ cups light cream
¾ cup light rum	1 cup sugar

Peel and slice pineapple. Core and cut all brown spots from each slice. Cut into small bite size pieces. Place in a large bowl and add ½ cup of rum. Toss with a fork. Cover and refrigerate several hours. Stir occasionally.

Preheat oven to 325° F.

Beat eggs in a large bowl. Add cream, ½ cup of sugar and remaining rum. Beat until blended.

Place remaining sugar in a small skillet over medium heat and cook, stirring occasionally, until sugar melts to a golden syrup.

Immediately pour syrup into bottom of 1½-quart ring mold and quickly tilt and rotate mold while syrup is still liquid to coat bottom and sides. Set aside until cool.

Beat egg mixture lightly and pour into mold.

Place mold in a shallow baking pan.

Pour sufficient hot water into baking pan to come halfway up sides of mold.

Place on middle rack of preheated oven and bake for 1 hour, or until a silver knife inserted in center of custard comes out clean. Remove mold from hot water and place on a rack. Cool, then refrigerate until chilled for 2 to 3 hours.

Unmold onto a serving platter. Caramelized sugar will run down sides.

Fill center with rum-soaked pineapple. Spoon syrup over pineapple and custard. Serve at once.

Serves 6 to 8.

NOTE: Mold can be made one day ahead, unmolded and assembled at the last minute.

Fresh Orange Ring with Whipped Cream Grand Marnier

This is delicious, easy to put together and good for you. No sugar is used—none at all.

3 envelopes unflavored gelatin	1 teaspoon grated orange rind
6 cups freshly squeezed, strained orange juice	2 tablespoons Grand Marnier or other orange-flavored liqueur
½ pint heavy cream	

Rinse a 6-cup ring mold or six 1-cup ring molds with cold water.

Sprinkle gelatin over 1 cup orange juice.

Heat remaining juice, but do not allow to boil. Add softened gelatin and stir over low heat until dissolved.

Pour into mold. Cool slightly, then refrigerate for several hours until firm.

Whip cream until stiff. Fold in grated orange rind and liqueur.

Turn orange ring out onto serving platter and fill center with whipped cream. Garnish with orange slices.

Serves 6.

VARIATIONS: Mixed, chopped, fresh fruit can be substituted for the flavored whipped cream, making this an elegant first course or main course salad for weight watchers.

Peach Melba Ring

2 3-ounce packages or 1
6-ounce package rasp-
berry gelatin
1 cup boiling water
2 cups dry white wine
½ cup cold water

1 10-ounce package
frozen peaches,
slightly thawed
1 10-ounce package
frozen raspberries,
slightly thawed
1 pint vanilla ice cream

Chill a 1½-quart ring mold.

Dissolve gelatin in boiling water. Add wine, cold water and frozen fruit. Stir gently until fruit thaws and separates. Gelatin may begin to thicken.

Rinse chilled mold with cold water. Pour in gelatin mixture. Chill until firm—4 hours or overnight.

Unmold. Just before serving, fill center of ring with scoops of ice cream.

Serves 6.

Creamy Rice Custard Ring with Strawberries

2 cups milk
¾ cup long grain con-
verted rice
1 teaspoon butter
¾ cup sugar
1 teaspoon vanilla
extract
⅛ teaspoon salt
2 envelopes unflavored
gelatin

¼ cup cold water
1 cup heavy cream
1 pint strawberries
¼ cup kirsch or
Cointreau
½ cup confectioners'
sugar

Heat milk in a saucepan. Add rice and butter. Simmer over low heat until rice is very soft. Add sugar, vanilla and salt. Stir until sugar has dissolved.

Sprinkle gelatin over cold water and let stand until soft. Stir softened gelatin into hot rice mixture. Pour entire mixture into container of electric blender. Blend for 10 seconds at low speed.

In a large mixing bowl beat cream until stiff. Fold into rice mixture.

Pour into 1½-quart mold that has been rinsed in cold water. Chill until firm (about 1½ hours).

Wash, hull and slice strawberries. Combine with kirsch or Cointreau and confectioners' sugar. Cover and let stand at room temperature for about 30 minutes, or until ready to serve.

To serve, unmold rice ring onto a round platter and fill center with strawberries.

Serves 6.

Riz à l'Impératrice (French Rice Cream Mold)

1½ cups milk
1 teaspoon butter
⅛ teaspoon salt
¾ cup long grain converted rice
4 egg yolks
¾ cup sugar
2 envelopes unflavored gelatin

¼ cup cold water
¼ cup brandy or orange liqueur
½ cup seedless raisins or ½ cup diced candied orange rind
1 cup heavy cream

Lightly grease a 2-quart ring mold with butter.

Combine milk, butter and salt in a saucepan and cook over medium heat until steamy hot. Add rice and simmer gently until very soft and liquid has been completely absorbed by rice. Transfer to a large mixing bowl.

In the top half of a double boiler beat egg yolks until smooth. Add sugar. Place over simmering water and beat with a rotary beater, electric hand mixer or wire whisk until very thick and about triple in volume.

Soften gelatin in cold water and stir into hot egg and sugar mixture. Beat until gelatin is dissolved. Add mixture to rice and blend well. Refrigerate until cool and slightly thickened.

While rice cools, pour brandy or liqueur over raisins or candied orange rind.

Beat cream until stiff.

Fold brandy- or liqueur-soaked fruit and whipped cream into cooled rice mixture.

Spoon into prepared mold and refrigerate until firm—2 to 4 hours.

Unmold onto chilled platter.

Serve with bottled Sauce Melba or fill center of mold with fresh strawberries sweetened and flavored with brandy or liqueur, or with any fresh fruit or fruit compote.

Serves 6.

OTHER SPECIALTIES

Charlotte Russe

14 ladyfingers, split
   lengthwise
Light rum, liqueur or fruit
   juice (about ¼ cup)
5 egg yolks
¾ cup sugar

2 envelopes unflavored
   gelatin
¼ cup light rum or any
   desired liqueur or fruit
   juice
½ cup milk
1 cup heavy cream

Line a 1½-quart Charlotte mold with ladyfingers. Begin at the bottom of the mold by placing a small round piece in the center. Cover the bottom completely with split ladyfingers, curved side down. To completely cover top, slice each into a long triangle and place the pointed tops toward the middle. Sprinkle lightly to barely moisten with rum, liqueur or fruit juice. Place more ladyfingers upright and close together around the sides of the mold.

Place egg yolks and sugar in top of a double boiler. Beat with a wire whisk over simmering water until about triple in volume.

Sprinkle gelatin over rum, liqueur or fruit juice to soften. Heat milk to boiling point. Add softened gelatin and stir until dissolved.

Beat cream until stiff. Fold in egg yolk mixture, then gelatin mixture.

Pour into lined mold. Chill until firm.

Unmold and, if desired, decorate with sweetened whipped cream.

Serves 6.

VARIATIONS: For CHARLOTTE AU CHOCOLAT, follow the recipe for CHARLOTTE RUSSE, adding two 1-ounce squares unsweetened chocolate to milk. Heat until chocolate is melted and proceed as directed.

Coeur à la Crème with Fraises au Kirsch

Classic individual coeur à la crème molds are available in many gourmet or French cooking equipment shops, but this absolutely beautiful and delicious dessert could also be made in any heart-shaped mold.

1 *pound cream-style cottage cheese*	2 *tablespoons confectioners' sugar*
1 *cup heavy cream*	FRAISES AU KIRSCH—see
¼ *teaspoon salt*	Sauces and Accompaniments

In a large mixing bowl mash cottage cheese with cream, salt and sugar until smooth. Use an old-fashioned potato masher or a heavy wooden spoon.

Pack the mixture into 6 individual coeur à la crème molds or a 1-quart heart-shaped mold. Place the molds on a cake rack which you have placed over a baking sheet. Refrigerate and allow to drain 6 to 8 hours.

If you do not have coeur à la crème molds, place the cheese mixture in a colander. Refrigerate and drain 8 hours or overnight. Next day line a heart-shaped metal mold with cheesecloth and pack the cheese mixture into it. Refrigerate until ready to serve, but no longer than 8 hours.

To serve, unmold coeur à la crème molds onto individual serving plates or unmold heart-shaped mold onto round platter and carefully remove cheesecloth. Surround with FRAISES AU KIRSCH, pouring a little of the liquid over each mold.

Serves 6.

FROZEN BOMBES
AND MOUSSES

One of the nicest things about frozen molded desserts—besides their great taste—is that they can be made as much as a week ahead and stored, tightly wrapped in foil, in the freezer until ready to make a gala ending to any dinner party. Inexpensive and easy to assemble, they can be varied with endless combinations of fruits, nuts, liqueurs and flavorings.

BOMBES

Chocolate Bombe Glacée with Peanut Brittle Mousse

1 pint chocolate ice cream	½ pound peanut brittle
	½ pint heavy cream

Chill a 1-quart decorative mold.

Let ice cream stand at room temperature until slightly soft. Spoon into chilled mold. Using the back of a wooden spoon, smooth the ice cream up the sides of the mold and press to form an even lining on bottom and sides, leaving the center hollow. Place in freezer.

Place the peanut brittle between two sheets of waxed paper on a chopping board. Crush with a rolling pin.

Beat cream until stiff. Fold in peanut brittle. Spoon into chocolate ice cream shell, filling mold to top.

Cover and seal top with foil, then wrap entire mold in foil. Freeze for several hours until firm.

About 1 hour before serving, unmold onto chilled serving platter. Refrigerate until time to serve.

Serves 4 to 6.

Pistachio Bombe Glacée with Cherry Mousse

1 pint pistachio ice cream	¼ pound candied cherries, finely chopped
¼ cup kirsch or Cherry Heering liqueur	½ pint heavy cream

Chill a 1-quart decorative mold.

Let ice cream stand at room temperature until slightly soft. Spoon into chilled mold. Using the back of a wooden spoon, smooth it up the sides of the mold and press to form an even lining on bottom and sides of mold, leaving the center hollow. Place in freezer.

Pour liqueur over chopped cherries in a small bowl. Let marinate at room temperature for 20 to 30 minutes.

Beat cream until stiff. Fold in cherries and liqueur.

Spoon into firm pistachio ice cream, filling mold to top. Cover top and seal with foil, then wrap entire mold in foil. Freeze for several hours until center is firm.

Unmold onto a chilled platter about 1 hour before serving. Refrigerate until time to serve.

Serves 4 to 6.

MOUSSES

Frozen Chocolate Rum Mousse (Super Quick and Easy)

2 cups heavy cream
½ cup chocolate syrup,
   canned

2 tablespoons dark
   Jamaican rum

Chill six 1-cup molds or custard cups.

Whip cream until stiff enough to mound softly on a spoon. Fold in chocolate syrup and rum.

Pour into prepared molds. Cover the top of each with foil, then wrap each tightly in foil. Freeze.

About 30 minutes before serving, unmold onto chilled, individual dessert plates. Refrigerate until time to serve. Garnish each serving with sweetened whipped cream and toasted slivered almonds.

Serves 6.

Frozen Kahlúa Chocolate Mousse

1 cup sugar
½ cup cocoa
½ cup water
¼ cup Kahlúa liqueur

1½ pints heavy cream
6 egg yolks
¼ teaspoon salt

Chill a 2-quart decorative mold.

Combine sugar and cocoa in a saucepan. Stir in water. Cook, stirring, until sugar melts. Then cook without stirring to soft ball stage (236°F. on a candy thermometer). Remove from heat and stir in Kahlúa. Set aside.

Beat cream until stiff. Set aside.

Beat egg yolks until pale and thick. Add salt. Add chocolate Kahlúa mixture, beating as it is added. Fold in whipped cream.

Spoon into chilled mold. Cover top of mold with foil and seal edges. Wrap entire mold tightly in foil. Freeze.

About 2 hours before serving, unmold onto a chilled platter. Refrigerate until time to bring to the table.

Serves 8.

Frozen Liqueur Mousse

6 *egg yolks*
½ *cup sugar*

4 *tablespoons desired liqueur such as crème de menthe, crème de cacao, cherry brandy, peach brandy, Cointreau, or Chartreuse*
1 *cup heavy cream*

Chill a 1-quart decorative mold.

Place egg yolks and sugar in the top half of a double boiler and beat with a wire whisk over simmering water until about triple in bulk. Remove from heat and cool to room temperature. Stir in liqueur.

In a large mixing bowl beat cream until stiff. Fold in egg yolk mixture.

Pour into chilled mold, cover and seal mold with foil. Then wrap entire mold tightly in foil. Freeze until about 1 hour before serving.

Unmold onto a chilled platter and refrigerate until time to serve.

Serves 6 to 8.

Frozen Mocha Mousse

6 egg yolks	2 tablespoons instant
1 cup sugar	coffee
4 ounces unsweetened	½ cup water
chocolate	1 cup heavy cream

Chill a 1½-quart decorative mold.

Place egg yolks and sugar in top half of a double boiler and beat with a wire whisk over simmering water until very thick and about triple in bulk. Remove from heat. Cool to room temperature.

Place chocolate, coffee and water in a saucepan and stir over low heat until chocolate has melted.

Fold chocolate mixture into egg yolk mixture.

In a large mixing bowl beat cream until stiff. Fold in chocolate-egg yolk mixture.

Pour into chilled mold. Cover and seal top of mold with foil, then wrap entire mold tightly in foil. Freeze until about 1 hour before serving.

Unmold onto a chilled platter and refrigerate until ready to serve.

Serves 6 to 8.

Frozen Vanilla Mousse

6 egg yolks	1 pint heavy cream
¾ cup sugar	HOT CHOCOLATE RUM SAUCE
½ teaspoon vanilla	—see Sauces and
extract	Accompaniments

Chill a 1-quart decorative mold.

Place egg yolks in the top of a double boiler and beat with a wire whisk until blended. Add the sugar and beat over barely simmering water until about triple in volume and mixture turns to a thick, creamy custard. Remove from heat and stir in vanilla.

Cover custard directly with plastic wrap and set aside until cooled to room temperature.

In a large mixing bowl beat cream until stiff. Fold in the cooled custard.

Pour into chilled mold. Cover and seal top of mold with foil, then wrap entire mold in foil. Freeze.

Unmold onto a chilled platter about 1 hour before serving. Refrigerate until time to serve.

Delicious served with HOT CHOCOLATE RUM SAUCE.

Serves 6 to 8.

VARIATIONS:

Frozen Applesauce Mousse

Chill a 1½-quart mold.

Follow the directions for VANILLA MOUSSE. Omit the vanilla. Flavor the mousse with 1 tablespoon apple brandy. Add 1 cup canned or bottled applesauce.

Frozen Peach Mousse

Chill a 1½-quart mold.

Follow the directions for VANILLA MOUSSE. Omit the vanilla and flavor instead with 1 tablespoon Calvados or applejack. Add 1 cup of puréed fresh peaches sweetened with about 2 tablespoons sugar to mousse mixture.

Garnish platter with sliced fresh peaches.

Frozen Pineapple Mousse

Chill a 1½-quart mold.

Follow the directions for VANILLA MOUSSE. Omit the vanilla and flavor the mousse with 1 tablespoon kirsch. Add 1 cup well-drained, canned, crushed pineapple.

SAUCES AND ACCOMPANIMENTS

Because mold cookery is almost always lazy day cookery, the hot and cold sauces and accompaniments that follow are all easy and quick to make. Nonetheless, they are delicious and I think you will find that they disprove the "would-be" gourmet's theory that sauces require special skill and hours of slow simmering to be worthy of the dish.

Crystal Clear Aspic

To line a decorative appetizer, entrée, or salad mold.

1¼ cup chicken, beef or
    fish stock or broth
1½ envelopes unflavored
    gelatin
 1 egg shell

1 egg white
2 tablespoons cognac,
    brandy, dry sherry or
    Madeira

Combine stock, gelatin, egg shell and egg white in a large saucepan. Bring to a full boil, stirring constantly. Remove from heat. Line a colander with several thicknesses of cheesecloth which have been rinsed in cold water and squeezed dry.

Strain the liquid through the cheesecloth into a large bowl. Add the liquor. Chill until mixture begins to thicken.

If aspic becomes firm before it is to be used, reheat to liquid and then chill to desired consistency.

NOTE: This recipe can be made ahead and stored in the refrigerator until needed as long as it is brought to a boil every 3 or 4 days to prevent spoilage.

MEAT AND VEGETABLE
SAUCES AND ACCOMPANIMENTS

Garlic Parsley Butter Sauce

Serve over fish mousse or vegetable timbales.

¼ pound butter
*2 cloves garlic, peeled
and cut in half
lengthwise*

½ cup minced parsley

Melt butter in top half of double boiler over low heat. Add garlic and place over simmering water for 5 to 10 minutes. Remove garlic. Add parsley and serve hot.

Makes about ½ cup.

Creole Sauce

For fish or chicken molds.

4 tablespoons butter
*1 small white onion,
peeled and minced*
*1 clove garlic, peeled
and minced*
*1 small green pepper,
seeded and finely
chopped*

*1 16-ounce can Italian-
style stewed tomatoes
with basil*
*1 tablespoon tomato
paste*
Salt
Pepper

Melt the butter in a saucepan over low heat. Add the onion, garlic and green pepper. Cook, stirring often, until vegetables are very limp. Add tomatoes and simmer for about 15 minutes. Stir in tomato paste and season to taste with salt and pepper. Continue to cook, stirring often, for about 10 minutes, or until sauce is thick.

Makes about 2 cups.

Cumberland Sauce

An excellent accompaniment to molded lamb or veal served hot or cold.

6 tablespoons currant jelly	½ teaspoon ground ginger
3 tablespoons Madeira	1 teaspoon prepared mustard
2 tablespoons lemon juice	1 teaspoon grated lemon rind

Place jelly and Madeira in a saucepan over low heat. Stir until jelly dissolves. Remove from heat and add remaining ingredients. Serve at room temperature.

Makes about ¾ cup.

Hollandaise Sauce
(Made Quickly in a Blender)

½ pound sweet butter	Dash of freshly ground white pepper
3 egg yolks	
1 tablespoon water	Dash of cayenne
Dash of salt	1 tablespoon lemon juice

Place butter in a small saucepan and cook over low heat until bubbly hot. Do not allow to brown.

Put all of the remaining ingredients in container of electric blender. Cover and set blender at high speed. Remove small cap for making additions while blender is running. Turn blender on and quickly add the melted butter in a steady stream. When all the butter has been added, turn off the motor.

Makes about 1½ cups.

NOTE: You can serve this HOLLANDAISE SAUCE hot or at room temperature. To hold it and still serve it hot, transfer it to the top of a double boiler and set aside at room temperature until ready to serve. Then reheat by placing over barely simmering water and stirring until very warm. Do not allow to overheat or boil.

VARIATION:

Sauce Maltaise

Add 1 teaspoon grated orange rind and ¼ cup freshly squeezed orange juice to 1½ cups HOLLANDAISE SAUCE.

Serve with ham mousse, spinach timbales, etc.

Horseradish Sauce for Meat

¼ cup fine dry bread
   crumbs
½ cup horseradish
1 tablespoon sugar

¼ teaspoon salt
½ cup milk
½ cup heavy cream

Place bread crumbs, horseradish, sugar and salt in a mixing bowl. Add milk and let stand until crumbs are soft. Beat cream until stiff. Fold into horseradish mixture. Chill before serving.

Makes about 2½ cups.

Sour Cream Horseradish Sauce

For cold jellied meat loaves and pâtés.

1 cup sour cream
¼ cup grated fresh horse-
radish (or substitute
bottled horseradish)

Pinch of salt

Blend well. Chill and serve.
Makes about 1¼ cups.

Tomato Horseradish Sauce

For fish or meat mold.

½ cup tomato catsup
3 tablespoons horse-
radish

1 tablespoon lemon juice
3 to 4 dashes Tabasco
sauce

Combine ingredients and mix well. Serve at room temperature.
Makes ½ cup sauce.

Hunter Sauce

For veal mousse or curried lamb loaf.

3 tablespoons butter
2 tablespoons minced
shallots
1 tablespoon flour
½ cup chicken stock
¼ cup dry white wine

1 8-ounce can tomato
sauce
1 small can sliced mush-
rooms, sautéed in
butter
Salt
Pepper

Melt the butter in a saucepan. Add the shallots and sauté until limp. Stir in the flour. When blended, slowly add the chicken stock and wine, stirring as they are added. Add tomato sauce and mushrooms. Season lightly with salt. Simmer gently for 15 to 20 minutes. Season with salt and pepper to taste.

Makes about 2 cups.

Lobster Sauce

For fish mold.

2 *tablespoons butter*	2 *tablespoons dry sherry*
2 *tablespoons flour*	1 *teaspoon lemon juice*
½ *cup bottled clam juice*	*Salt*
1 *cup light cream*	1 *cup cooked, diced*
2 *egg yolks*	*lobster meat*

Melt the butter in a saucepan over low heat. Stir in the flour. When smooth, slowly add clam juice, stirring as it is added. Slowly stir in the cream. Cook, stirring, until mixture begins to thicken to a smooth sauce. Remove from heat.

In a small bowl beat egg yolks until well blended, then beat in sherry and lemon juice. Add a few tablespoons of the sauce and beat well. Pour this into the remaining sauce. Return the pan to low heat, salt to taste, and stir until thick and smooth. Add the lobster. Serve hot.

Makes about 2½ cups.

NOTE: To hold sauce until serving time, set the pan of sauce in a pan of cold water for a few seconds to stop the cooking process. Remove and cover surface of sauce directly with plastic wrap. Set sauce aside at room temperature until ready to use. Reheat just before serving over simmering water. Stir constantly until steamy hot, but do not allow to boil.

Mayonnaise-based Sauces

Here are several mayonnaise-based sauces for cold mousses, aspics or salads. Use top quality, commercially prepared real mayonnaise and I think you will find them truly appetizing and delicious.

Anchovy Dressing

½ cup mayonnaise
2 tablespoons cream or
   milk

1 2-ounce can anchovy
   fillets, finely chopped

Mix all ingredients well. Chill before serving.
  Makes about ¾ cups.
  Use for fish molds or any unsweet vegetable mold or salad.

Quick Sauce Andalouse

Serve with chicken or fish mousse, cheese timbales, molded salads, etc.

¼ cup tomato catsup
2 cups mayonnaise
2 tablespoons lemon
   juice

3–4 dashes Tabasco sauce
2 tablespoons finely
   minced chives or tops
   of green onions

Combine all ingredients. Chill for use with cold mousses. For hot mousses, heat in top of double boiler over simmering water.
  Makes about 2½ cups.

Deviled Mayonnaise

Serve with cold fish mousse.

1 cup mayonnaise
1 tablespoon mustard
¼ cup tomato catsup
2 teaspoons tarragon
  vinegar

1 teaspoon Worcester-
  shire sauce
2–3 drops Tabasco sauce
½ cup sour cream
Salt

Combine ingredients and chill thoroughly.
  Makes about 2½ cups.

Hot Mayonnaise Caper Sauce

A zesty sauce for vegetable timbales.

1 cup mayonnaise

¼ cup well-drained
  capers, coarsely
  chopped

Combine and heat in top of double boiler over simmering water
until heated through.
  Makes about 1¼ cups.

Italian Mayonnaise

For molded vegetable salads.

3 tablespoons Italian-
  style salad dressing

1 cup mayonnaise
¼ cup minced chives

Stir salad dressing into mayonnaise. Blend. Place in serving
bowl and sprinkle with chives.
  Makes about 1½ cups.

Mayonnaise Colée
(Gelatin Mayonnaise)

2 tablespoons dry white
  wine
1 tablespoon lemon juice
2 tablespoons chicken or
  beef stock, clam juice
  or tomato juice

1 envelope unflavored
  gelatin
2 cups commercially
  prepared or very thick
  homemade mayonnaise

Combine wine, lemon juice and stock or juice in top half of
a double boiler. Sprinkle gelatin over surface and let stand about
5 minutes to soften. Stir over simmering water until gelatin dissolves. Let cool to lukewarm. Fold in the mayonnaise. Taste for
seasoning. Add salt, if desired.

Use just before mixture sets for coating cold molded dishes
such as ham mousse or molded salads.

Makes about 4 cups.

Sauce Romanoff

For piquant gelatin salads, and especially for cold seafood
molds or mousses.

1 cup mayonnaise
1 tablespoon lemon juice
1 tablespoon horseradish

½ cup sour cream
1 small jar red or black
  caviar

Mix together all ingredients except caviar. Chill.

Gently stir in caviar just before serving.

Makes about 2 cups.

VARIATION: Well-drained, chopped capers are an excellent substitute for the caviar. They are almost as elegant and much less
expensive.

Roquefort Cream Mayonnaise

Serve with meat aspics or jellied vegetable salads.

½ cup heavy cream	1 cup mayonnaise
2 tablespoons Roquefort cheese	

Whip cream until stiff. Add crumbled cheese. Fold in mayonnaise. Chill well.
Makes about 2½ cups.

Sauce Suèdoise

Delicious served with ham mousse.

1 cup mayonnaise	1 tablespoon horseradish
½ cup canned applesauce	1 teaspoon sugar

Combine ingredients and blend well. Chill.
Makes about 1½ cups.

Tartar Sauce

Serve with cold fish mousse or any vegetable aspic salad.

1 cup mayonnaise	1 tablespoon finely minced mixed sweet pickles
1 tablespoon tarragon vinegar	
1 tablespoon capers, well-drained	1 teaspoon grated onion

Mix well and chill.
Makes about 1¼ cups.

Alexander's Tartar Sauce

For molded fish and seafood dishes.

1 tablespoon each onion,
sour pickle, capers and
parsley, all finely
minced
1 chopped, hard-cooked
egg yolk

2 cups mayonnaise
¼ cup cider vinegar
1 teaspoon prepared
mustard
Salt

Combine in a mixing bowl the minced onion, pickle, capers, parsley and chopped egg yolk. Stir in mayonnaise.

Heat vinegar just to boiling, add to mayonnaise mixture and blend well. Stir in mustard and season to taste with salt.

Makes about 2½ cups.

Whipped Cream Mayonnaise

½ cup heavy cream
¼ cup mayonnaise

⅛ teaspoon salt

Whip cream. Fold in mayonnaise and salt.
Makes about 1¼ cups.

Mornay Sauce

For ham and vegetable timbales and for molded vegetable dishes.

2 tablespoons butter
2 tablespoons flour
1 cup chicken stock
½ cup milk
1 egg yolk, lightly
beaten

¼ cup grated Emmenthal
or Swiss cheese
¼ cup dry white wine
Salt
Pepper

Melt the butter in a saucepan over low heat. Stir in the flour. When blended, slowly add the stock, stirring as it is added. Stir in the milk and cook, stirring constantly, until sauce begins to thicken. Beat a little of the hot sauce into the beaten egg and quickly stir this mixture into the remaining sauce. Add the cheese and wine and cook, stirring until sauce is thick and smooth. Season with salt and pepper to taste.

Makes about 2 cups.

Mushroom Sauce

A classic sauce that will do justice to many molded dishes, such as chicken mousse, ham loaf, fish pudding and vegetable or cheese timbales.

3 tablespoons butter	2 tablespoons flour
1 teaspoon minced scallions	1½ cups milk—or part milk, part chicken
½ cup sliced raw mushrooms	stock
2 tablespoons Madeira or sherry	Salt

Melt 1 tablespoon of butter in a saucepan. Add scallions and sauté until limp. Add mushrooms and cook over very low heat, stirring often, for about 15 minutes. Pour in Madeira or sherry. Raise the heat and stir until the wine is cooked away entirely.

Add remaining butter. When melted, stir in flour. Slowly add milk, stirring as added. Cook, stirring, until sauce is thick. Salt to taste.

Makes about 1½ cups.

Mushroom Sour Cream Sauce

A delicious sauce for timbales or a hot mousse.

8 to 10 large fresh
   mushrooms
6 tablespoons butter
2 tablespoons flour
1 cup chicken stock

½ cup sour cream
2 tablespoons dry sherry
   (optional)
Salt

Trim the mushrooms and slice them diagonally. Melt 3 tablespoons of butter in a saucepan over low heat. Add the mushrooms
and sauté for 10 to 15 minutes. Then add remaining butter. Stir in
the flour, then slowly add the chicken stock, stirring as it is added.
Cook, stirring, over low heat until sauce begins to thicken. Stir
in sour cream and sherry. Season to taste with salt. Serve very
hot, but do not allow to boil after adding sour cream.
   Makes about 2 cups.

Mustard Sauce

For meat molds and pâtés.

½ cup heavy cream
½ cup mayonnaise

1 tablespoon prepared
   mustard
⅛ teaspoon salt

Whip cream until stiff. Fold in remaining ingredients.
   Makes about 1¼ cups.

Hot Mustard Sauce

For cold meat aspics and pâtés.

¼ cup dry mustard   *Pinch turmeric*
½ cup stale beer

Blend well and serve at room temperature.
Makes about ¾ cup.

Shrimp Sauce

The quintessence of elegance. Serve this rich sauce with any hot molded fish dish; or, for something special, with vegetable or cheese timbales.

½ pound raw shrimp,   *2 tablespoons flour*
   shelled and deveined   *2 cups light cream*
3 tablespoons butter   *3 well-beaten egg yolks*
¼ cup dry sherry   Salt

Place the shrimp, 1 tablespoon of butter and the sherry in a small skillet. Cook, stirring gently, over moderate heat until shrimp turn pink—1 to 2 minutes.

In a saucepan over low heat, melt the remaining butter. Stir in the flour. When blended slowly add the cream, stirring as it is added. Cook, stirring until smooth. Stir a little of the sauce into the egg yolks and add this mixture to the rest of the sauce, stirring rapidly as it is added. Add the shrimp, butter and sherry. Continue to cook, stirring until sauce is thick and smooth.

Makes about 3 cups.

NOTE: Sauce may be made 1 to 2 hours ahead. Cover surface of sauce with plastic wrap. Set aside at room temperature. Remove plastic wrap and reheat just before serving.

Sauce Smitane

For ham loaf or chicken timbales.

2 *tablespoons butter*	2 *tablespoons Madeira*
2 *tablespoons minced*	1 *teaspoon lemon juice*
shallots	*Salt*
½ *cup chicken stock*	*Pepper*
2 *cups sour cream*	

Melt butter in a heavy saucepan. Add shallots and sauté until limp. Add stock and simmer over medium heat until reduced to about half (about 15 minutes). Stir in sour cream and cook, stirring constantly, until sauce is steamy hot. Add Madeira, then lemon juice. Cook, stirring, a final 3 to 4 minutes. Season to taste with salt and pepper.

Makes about 2½ cups.

Quick and Easy Basic Beef or Chicken Stock

While nothing can make a molded dish (or any dish) quite as delicious as slowly cooked, carefully prepared homemade stock, there are satisfactory and less time consuming substitutes. Canned beef and chicken stock broth or bouillon can be quickly given homemade flavor (and the taste of the preservatives used concealed) by a bit of simmering with a few fresh vegetables plus a little wine.

This recipe can be used whenever a molded dish in this book requires stock in its recipe. It can also be used for aspics and as the base for many sauces.

2 13-ounce cans un-
diluted chicken or
beef stock
Leafy tops from 2 or 3
stalks celery
1 small onion, peeled
and coarsely chopped
1 or 2 cloves garlic,
peeled and cut in half
lengthwise

2–3 sprigs parsley
1 bay leaf
Pinch dried thyme
½ cup dry white wine or
dry vermouth
¼ to ½ cup chopped
fresh mushroom stems
(optional; save the
caps to be used in a
more "showy" way)

Combine ingredients in a saucepan and simmer slowly for about 1 hour. Cool slightly, then strain through a fine sieve.

Makes about 3 cups stock.

NOTE: This recipe can be made weeks ahead and frozen, or if refrigerated it must be brought to a boil every 3 or 4 days to prevent spoilage. Reheat before using.

Tomato Catsup Sauce

Use with pâtés or jellied meat.

2 tablespoons butter
1 clove garlic, peeled
and cut in half length-
wise
1 tablespoon flour
½ cup tomato catsup
¼ cup dry sherry
2 tablespoons red wine
vinegar

½ cup chicken or beef
stock
1 teaspoon brown sugar
1 teaspoon prepared
mustard
Salt
Pepper

Combine first nine ingredients in saucepan and bring to boil over medium heat. Lower heat and simmer very gently for 5 minutes. Remove and discard garlic. Season with salt and pepper. Chill thoroughly before serving.

Makes about 1½ cups.

Creamy Tomato Sauce

What could be easier—or better? Use over vegetable timbales, fish mousses, rice or pasta rings, etc.

1 tablespoon butter	Salt
1 tablespoon flour	Freshly ground black
½ cup milk	pepper
1 8-ounce Italian-style tomato sauce	

Melt the butter in a heavy saucepan over moderate heat. Stir in flour. Remove from heat and slowly add the milk, stirring as it is added. Then cook, stirring constantly, until thick. Pour in the tomato sauce and stir until mixture is smooth. If the sauce is too thick, add a little additional milk. Season to taste with salt and pepper.

Makes about 2 cups.

Quick and Easy Tomato Sauce

Who said a really good tomato sauce must simmer for hours? It's not always so. This sauce takes no more than a few minutes work-time and less than a half hour of unsupervised cooking.

1 tablespoon butter	2 tablespoons tomato paste
2 tablespoons minced onion	1 bay leaf
2 cloves garlic, unpeeled	2 tablespoons dry white wine or dry vermouth
1 16-ounce can stewed tomatoes	Salt
	Pepper

Melt the butter in a saucepan. Add the onion and sauté u limp. Add remaining ingredients and season lightly with salt

pepper. Simmer gently for about 30 minutes. Remove and discard garlic. Season to taste.

Makes about 4 cups.

Quick and Easy Véronique Sauce

Absolutely divine served over any fish mousse.

¼ pound butter	1 cup seedless grapes
½ cup white wine	

Combine ingredients and simmer over low heat for about 10 minutes.

Makes about 2 cups sauce.

Creamy Vinaigrette Sauce

Serve with jellied vegetable salads.

1 egg yolk	1 tablespoon minced
3 tablespoons wine	green onion
vinegar	Dash Tabasco sauce
1 teaspoon mustard	Salt
¼ teaspoon paprika	Pepper
	1 cup salad oil

In a mixing bowl combine the egg yolk, vinegar, mustard, paprika and green onion. Add Tabasco, salt and pepper to taste. Beat with a wire whisk for about 2 minutes until about double in bulk. Add the oil slowly, beating constantly as it is added.

Makes about 2 cups.

Country-style Buttermilk Ring

Serve with cold meats.

2 *envelopes unflavored gelatin*	1 *tablespoon cider vinegar*
¼ *cup cold water*	½ *teaspoon dry mustard*
¾ *cup boiling water*	1 *tablespoon minced onion*
2 *cups buttermilk*	
1 *cup chili sauce*	¾ *cup finely chopped celery*
2 *teaspoons sugar*	
1 *teaspoon salt*	¼ *cup finely chopped green pepper*
3–4 *drops Tabasco sauce*	

Chill a 1½-quart ring mold.

Sprinkle gelatin over cold water in a large mixing bowl. Let stand a minute to soften. Pour in boiling water and stir until gelatin is dissolved. Add buttermilk, chili sauce, sugar, salt, Tabasco, vinegar and mustard, and blend well. Chill until thickened. Fold in remaining ingredients.

Rinse chilled mold with cold water. Pour in buttermilk mixture. Chill until firm.

Unmold and fill center with coleslaw or mixed cooked vegetable salad.

Serves 6.

NOTE: This is another of those very "adaptable to what's on hand" recipes. You can use sour cream instead of buttermilk, catsup instead of chili sauce, lemon juice instead of vinegar. If you like, use all celery instead of celery and green pepper. And, of course, you can season to taste.

Molded Mint Jelly

Serve with hot or cold lamb, or with any cold meat platter.

¾ cup chopped fresh mint leaves	¼ cup cider vinegar
1½ cups boiling water	½ cup sugar
1 envelope unflavored gelatin	2–3 drops green food coloring

Rinse four ½-cup molds in cold water and refrigerate until ready to use.

In a mortar or heavy bowl crush mint leaves using a pestle, an old-fashioned potato masher or a heavy wooden spoon. Transfer crushed leaves to a tea pot. Pour in boiling water. Cover pot and let mixture steep for about 5 minutes.

Sprinkle gelatin over vinegar and let stand until softened.

Strain hot mint liquid over softened gelatin. Add sugar and stir until gelatin and sugar have dissolved.

Stir in food coloring. Pour into chilled molds and refrigerate until firm.

Serves 4.

Molded Vegetable Relish

Excellent with cold molded turkey or chicken salads.

1 3-ounce package lemon or lime gelatin	2 tablespoons vinegar
¾ teaspoon salt	2 teaspoons grated onion
1 cup boiling water	Dash of pepper
¾ cup unsweetened apple juice	

Vegetable combinations:
—½ cup each finely chopped cabbage, celery, and carrots, and 3 tablespoons finely chopped green pepper

—¾ cup each finely chopped cabbage and celery, ¼ cup finely chopped green pepper, and 2 tablespoons diced pimento

—¾ cup each finely chopped cabbage and celery, ½ cup chopped pickle, and 2 tablespoons diced pimento

—¾ cup each drained cooked peas and diced celery and ½ cup finely chopped cabbage

—1 cup finely chopped cabbage, ½ cup sliced stuffed olives, and omit the salt

—⅔ cup grated carrots and ¼ cup finely chopped green pepper.

Chill a 1½-quart decorative mold.

Dissolve gelatin and salt in boiling water. Add apple juice, vinegar, grated onion and pepper. Chill until thickened. Fold in vegetable combination.

Rinse chilled mold with cold water. Pour in thickened gelatin mixture. Chill until firm—about 3 hours.

Unmold. For salad, serve with crisp lettuce and garnish with mayonnaise, if desired.

Makes 6 to 8 servings.

Champagne Sour Cream Mousse

Serve with cold meats.

2 tablespoons un-
    flavored gelatin
	2 tablespoons prepared
	    mustard

⅓ cup cold water	¼ cup minced chives
2 cups sour cream	¼ cup well-drained,
½ cup dry champagne	chopped pimento

Lightly grease a 1-quart mold.

Sprinkle gelatin over cold water to soften. Set aside.

Heat sour cream in top of double boiler over simmering water to steamy hot. Stir almost constantly. Do not allow to boil. Stir in softened gelatin and continue to stir until completely dissolved.

Remove from heat and let cool slightly. Add champagne, mustard, chives and pimento. Blend well.

Pour into prepared mold. Cover and refrigerate several hours until firmly set.

Unmold just before serving.
Serves 6.

Glazed Carrots and Onions

8 *very small white onions, peeled*	2 *tablespoons butter*
4–6 *medium to large carrots, scraped and cut into thick slices*	½ *cup water*
	1 *tablespoon sugar*
	½ *teaspoon salt*

Place onions in a saucepan and cover with water. Bring to a full boil, reduce heat and simmer for 2 to 3 minutes. Drain.

Place drained onions and remaining ingredients in a saucepan over low heat. Cover with a tightly fitting lid and steam 20 to 25 minutes, until vegetables are tender and liquid is completely reduced.

Uncover as little as possible (only to make sure liquid has not evaporated) before vegetables are tender. Add a little additional water only if necessary.

Makes 4 servings.

Peas and Onions in Tomato Sauce

6 *small white onions, peeled*	1 *10-ounce package frozen peas*
1 *tablespoon butter*	CREAMY TOMATO SAUCE— see p. 189

Place onions in a saucepan. Add water to cover by about 1 inch. Bring to a full boil and boil 5 minutes. Drain. Cover with fresh water and simmer until tender. Drain off water. Add butter, peas and tomato sauce to pot. Simmer until peas are tender.

Makes 4 servings.

Pickled Shrimp Filling

For BLOODY MARY RING MOLD.

¾ cup cider vinegar
3 or 4 fresh green chili
    peppers
1½ cups salad oil
1 teaspoon salt

1 teaspoon sugar
½ teaspoon freshly
    ground black pepper
2 pounds shrimp, boiled,
    shelled and deveined

Pour vinegar into a widemouthed jar (one with a lid). Cut peppers lengthwise, discard seeds and add to the vinegar. Cover and refrigerate several days. This makes pepper vinegar, a great hot seasoning.

Combine pepper vinegar with oil, salt, sugar and pepper, and pour over shrimp in a nonmetal bowl. Refrigerate several hours. Drain and spoon into center of ring mold.

DESSERT SAUCES
AND ACCOMPANIMENTS

Blueberry Sauce

For FOURTH OF JULY CHERRY FIRECRACKERS.

1 10-ounce package frozen blueberries or 1½ cups fresh blueberries
2 tablespoons red currant jelly
3 tablespoons cold water
2 tablespoons lemon juice
1 tablespoon kirsch or brandy
½ teaspoon cornstarch

Combine all ingredients in a small saucepan and cook over low heat, stirring often, until berries have softened and sauce is slightly thickened. Cool to room temperature before serving.

Makes about 2½ cups.

Bourbon Sauce

Serve hot or cold over BOURBON PUDDING.

1 cup bourbon whiskey   ½ cup honey

Combine in top of a double boiler. Bring to a boil over medium heat, then place over simmering water and cook, stirring constantly, for 3 to 5 minutes.

Makes about 1½ cups.

Hot Chocolate Rum Sauce

Serve hot over FROZEN VANILLA MOUSSE.

12 squares semi-sweet	¾ cup water
chocolate (12 ounces)	¼ cup light rum

Combine ingredients and stir in top of double boiler over simmering water until chocolate has dissolved.
Makes about 1¼ cups.

Fraises au Kirsch for Rice Ring

1 pint large, fresh ripe	½ cup confectioners'
strawberries	sugar
	¼ cup kirsch

Hull strawberries, place in a colander and quickly rinse under cold water. Blot dry and slice. Place in a nonmetal bowl. Add sugar and kirsch. Toss lightly. Cover and let stand at room temperature for about 1 hour before serving. Or prepare several hours ahead and refrigerate, bringing to room temperature before serving.
Makes about 2¼ cups.

Caramel Coconut Icing for Bunny or Lamb Mold

⅓ cup milk	1½ cups confectioners'
2 cups brown sugar	sugar (approximately)
6 tablespoons butter	1 to 1½ cups coconut
	Raisins and candy drops

Put milk, sugar and butter in a saucepan and stir over medium heat until sugar is dissolved and butter melted. Cool slightly. Stir in sufficient confectioners' sugar to make a smooth, thick icing.

Ice cake and cover with coconut, pressing it over entire surface. Use raisins for eyes and candy drops for nose and mouth.

Santa Icing

1 *unbeaten egg white*	*Red and green food*
2 *to 2¼ cups confec-*	*coloring*
tioners' sugar	*Cloves, raisins or candy*
1 *teaspoon lemon juice*	*drops*

Add egg white gradually to confectioners' sugar, stirring with a wooden spoon until smooth and shiny. Add lemon juice. Divide into three bowls. Stir red food coloring into one, green into the second and leave third portion white.

Ice "à la Santa." Use cloves, raisins or candy drops for eyes, nose and mouth.

Hard Sauce Shells

Used to decorate steamed Christmas puddings or any steamed pudding.

¼ *pound butter at room*	1 *tablespoon heavy*
temperature	*cream*
1¼ *cup confectioners'*	1 *tablespoon cognac or*
sugar (approximately)	*good brandy*

Cream the butter until smooth and fluffy. Gradually add about 1 cup of sugar. Beat in cream and cognac. Add additional sugar as needed to make a stiff, firm sauce.

Pack into 12 Madeleine shells. Chill.

To unmold, loosen each shell with the tip of a silver knife. It should come out easily. If not, turn plaque upside down and cover with a kitchen towel that has been wrung out in hot water. Loosen edges again with a silver knife. Shells should come out in elegant shape.

Makes 12.

SUGGESTED MENUS

BRIDGE LUNCHEON SPECIAL

Recipes for asterisked dishes appear in this book.

Rice Timbales with Swiss Cheese*

Creamed Peas   Broiled Peach Halves

Hot Rolls

Frozen Pineapple Mousse*

Crisp Cookies

EASTER SUNDAY LUNCH

Stuffed "Easter" Eggs
(Stuff eggs, press halves together and
hold with a cocktail pick in bed
of finely shredded lettuce)

Baked Ham with Glazed Peach Halves

Broccoli Walnut Ring Mold*
Filled with Creamed Tiny Peas

Hot Crusty Rolls

Dry White Wine

Easter Bunny Cake*
with Coconut Icing*

EASY BUDGET LUNCHEON FOR SIX

Timbales au Petits Pois*
with Mushroom Sauce*

Mixed Green Salad

Cornbread Squares

Dry White Wine

Steamed Chocolate Pudding
with Whipped Cream

INFORMAL LUNCH ON THE TERRACE

Prosciutto or Westphalian Ham
with Melon

Pâté Maison*

Crusty French Bread

Dry White Wine

Fresh Peaches or Strawberries with Kirsch

Lace Cookies

Coffee

LUNCH FOR A CROWD
(Entirely Prepared Ahead)

Country Pâté*
Potato Salad with Dill and Celery Seed
Cranberry Apple Salad Mold*
Garlic French Bread
California Mountain Red Wine
Baked Apples with Cognac and Sour Cream

LUNCHEON WITH AN INDIAN ACCENT

Rice Pilaf Ring*
Filled with Curried Chicken

Crisp Bread Sticks

Dry White Wine

Fresh Fruit Compote
of Melon, Peaches, Strawberries
(Whatever fresh fruit is in season)
with
Grand Marnier Liqueur

SPECIAL LUNCHEON FOR SPECIAL GUESTS

Classic Tomato Aspic Ring*
Filled with Shrimp or Chicken Salad

Dry White Wine

Thin Bread, Butter
and
Watercress Sandwich

Fresh Pineapple with
Vanilla Ice Cream and Kirsch

WARM WEATHER LUNCHEON FOR SIX
(Made Ahead)

Molded Spanish Tuna Salad*
with Mayonnaise
Garnished with Avocado Slices
Fresh Pineapple and Ripe Olives

Crusty French Rolls

Brie Cheese

Barbados Chocolate Pudding*

WINTER LUNCH FOR SIX

*Ham Timbales
with Mushroom Sauce**

Tomato Halves Broiled with Currant Jelly

Corn Sticks

Dry White Wine

*Classic Orange Mousse**

WINTER LUNCHEON FOR SIX

*Hot Tomato and Hot Split Pea Soups
(Canned varieties laced with sherry)*

*Cheese Timbales**

Creamed Green Beans Amandine

Corn Sticks

Dry White Wine

*Steamed Cranberry Pudding**

DINNER FOR A SPRING EVENING

*Cold Ham Mousse
with Mustard Mayonnaise**

Fresh Asparagus   Steamed New Potatoes

Hot Parkerhouse Rolls

Stewed Rhubarb with Strawberries and Sour Cream

DINNER WITH A FRENCH ACCENT

Jellied Consomme Madrilène
Garnished with Chopped Black Olives and Parsley

Mousse de Veau*
Garnished with Creamed Carrots and Onions Watercress

French Bread

Dry White Wine

Caramel Crisp Ring*
with Fresh Fruit

DINNER WITH AN ITALIAN ACCENT

Antipasto of Tomatoes, Olives,
Pimentos and Cold Roast Peppers

Italian Lamb and Eggplant Mold*

Steamed Brown Rice
with Slivered Almonds and Raisins

Fresh Orange Ring
with Whipped Cream*

DINNER WITH A NEW ENGLAND ACCENT

Cold Tunafish Mousse*
with Mustard Sauce*

Boston Baked Beans
(Canned variety with the flavor
stepped up with mustard and
brown sugar)

Classic Boston Brown Bread*

Dry White Wine

Suggested Menus

*Stewed Apple Quarters
with Rum and Heavy Cream*

DINNER WITH A MEXICAN ACCENT

Guacamole Dip with Corn Chips

Polenta Ring
Filled with Chili and Topped
with Shredded Lettuce and Grated
Sharp Cheese*

*Salad of Mild Purple Onion
Rings and Orange Sections
with French Dressing*

Mexican Beer

Jamaican Flan Ring*

DINNER WITH A SCANDINAVIAN ACCENT

*Pickled Herring
with Chives and Watercress*

Norgwegian Fiskepudding
with Creamy Tomato Sauce**

Steamed New Potatoes

*Mixed Green Salad
with
Capers and Celery Seed and French Dressing*

Cold Imported Beer

*Crisp Apple Slices with Danish Cheese
Unsalted Crackers*

AN ELEGANT BUT EASY DINNER FOR SIX

Black Bean Soup
with Sherry and a Lemon Slice in
Each Soup Plate

*Mousse de Poisson Amandine**
*with Shrimp Sauce**
Minted Tiny Peas   Steamed Brown Rice
Hot Crusty Rolls

Dry White Wine

Fresh Pineapple with Kirsch

FESTIVE BUT INEXPENSIVE DINNER FOR EIGHT

Cold Broccoli Vinaigrette

*Ham Loaf**
*with Horseradish Sauce**

Whole Baby Carrots

Small New Potatoes with Parsley

Dry White Wine

*Steamed Cranberry Pudding**

SKY'S THE LIMIT DINNER

*Shrimp and Avocado Mousse**
Garnished with Cucumber and Tomato Slices

Broiled Sirloin Steak

*Potatoes Anna**

Broiled Tomato Halves
(Topped with onion ring
and a teaspoon of currant jelly before broiling)

Suggested Menus

Cold Asparagus Vinaigrette

Toasted French Bread Slices

Red Bordeaux or California Mountain Red

*Pistachio Bombe Glacée with Cherry Mousse**

SUPER BUDGET DINNER

*Creamy Codfish Mold**
with
*Tomato Horseradish Sauce**

*Glazed Carrots and Onions**

Spinach Salad with
Crumbled Bacon Bits

Dry White Wine

*Creole Pineapple Pudding**

BUFFET FOR TEN

*Cold Braised Beef in Wine Aspic**

Mixed Cooked Vegetable Salad Vinaigrette

Macaroni Salad with Anchovies
and Pimento Strips

California Mountain Red Wine
or French Bordeaux

Hot French Rolls

*Steamed Chocolate Pudding**

BUFFET PARTY FOR A SUMMER EVENING

*Chicken Liver Pâté in Aspic**

*Cold Fish Mold**
*with Alexander's Tartar Sauce**

Fromage à la Crème   *Mixed Green Salad with Anchovies*

California Champagne

Assorted Rolls and Crackers

Fresh Peaches in Champagne

CHRISTMAS DESSERT AND COFFEE BUFFET
(Easily Made Ahead)

*Santa Claus Cake**

*Old-Fashioned Christmas Pudding**
with Brandied Hard Sauce

*Riz à l'Impératrice**
*with Fraises au Kirsch**

Espresso Coffee   *Regular Coffee*

A Choice of Liqueurs:
Crème de Ménthe   *Grand Marnier*
Pernod

EASY ON THE BUDGET BUFFET

*Fromage à la Crème**
Unsalted Crackers

*Turkey Ring Mold**   *Brown Rice Ring*
*with Cumberland Sauce**   *with Vegetables**

*Steamed Spinach Soufflé**

*Cold Broccoli Vinaigrette with
Anchovy and Pimento Strips*

Tray of Assorted Hot Rolls

*Dry White Wine or
A Good Cold Imported Beer*

Blackberry Pudding
with Whipped Cream*

AN ELEGANT BRUNCH BUFFET

Fresh Orange Ring
Filled with Fresh Strawberries,
Orange Sections or Fresh Pineapple*

Brunch Timbales*

*Little Link Sausages   Broiled Canadian Bacon
(Sprinkle with a
little brown sugar
before broiling)*

*Hot Southern-style Grits
with Plenty of Butter*

Hot Biscuits   Miniature Danish Pastries

Orange Blossoms   or   Champagne

Coffee

FOURTH OF JULY PORCH BUFFET

Spiced Cider Ham Loaf
Spanish Tuna Salad Mold**

Cucumber Sour Cream Mold*

Corn on the Cob

*Bowl of Cherry Tomatoes
with Mustard Sauce**

Cold Beer

*Fourth of July Cherry Firecrackers**

WEDDING RECEPTION BUFFET

*Curried Pâté**   *Turkey and Smithfield*
Unsalted Crackers   *Ham in Aspic**

*Halibut Mousse**
*with Lobster Sauce**

Tiny Finger Sandwiches
(Minced Watercress and Butter,
Chicken Salad,
Chopped Ripe Olive)

*Coeur à la Crème with Fraises au Kirsch**

Wedding Cake
and
Pastel Petits Fours
(Both from a good bakery)

Champagne

INDEX